CW01511927

VEGAN SLOW COOKER COOKBOOK

ANDREA J. CLARK

© Copyright 2017 by Andrea J. Clark. All rights reserved.

The following eBook is reproduced below with the goal of providing information that is as accurate and as reliable as possible. Regardless, purchasing this eBook can be seen as consent to the fact that both the publisher and the author of this book are in no way experts on the topics discussed within, and that any recommendations or suggestions made herein are for entertainment purposes only. Professionals should be consulted as needed before undertaking any of the action endorsed herein.

This declaration is deemed fair and valid by both the American Bar Association and the Committee of Publishers Association and is legally binding throughout the United States.

Furthermore, the transmission, duplication or reproduction of any of the following work, including precise information, will be considered an illegal act, irrespective whether it is done electronically or in print. The legality extends to creating a secondary or tertiary copy of the work or a recorded copy and is only allowed with an express written consent of the Publisher. All additional rights are reserved.

The information in the following pages is broadly considered to be a truthful and accurate account of facts, and as such any inattention, use or misuse of the information in question by the reader will render any resulting actions solely under their purview. There are no scenarios in which the publisher or the original author of this work can be in any fashion deemed liable for any hardship or damages that may befall them after undertaking information described herein.

Additionally, the information found on the following pages is intended for informational purposes only and should thus be considered, universal. As befitting its nature, the information presented is without assurance regarding its continued validity or interim quality. Trademarks that mentioned are done without written consent and can in no way be considered an endorsement from the trademark holder.

CONTENTS

INTRODUCTION

I can't tell you how often people say to me, "I have a slow cooker, but I never use it." Well, I have to tell you that this is going to change after you read this cookbook. Slow cooking is one of the most wonderful ways of cooking. There are countless amazing slow cooker recipes waiting for you to try, and with a little bit of planning, this kitchen tool can save you so much valuable time.

For most of us, our evenings are busy. We'd rather spend more time with our family than spending a few hours in the kitchen. With a slow cooker, all you need is a bit of the morning planning. Just throw all the ingredients in the slow cooker before leaving the house and be prepared to be greeted by the scents from your slow cooker when you come home in the evening. How awesome is that?

Now, why do I want to write a vegan cookbook?

People who consume a plant-based diet, or vegans, are often seen as fringe eaters that have an unnatural passion for the rights of animals, but a vegan diet can be more than that. While a lot of vegans do view animal rights passionately, it is important for you to start seeing a vegan lifestyle beyond animal rights.

As far as nutrition goes, a vegan lifestyle will provide you diet full of healthy foods like soy products, beans, nuts, whole grains, vegetables, and fruits. You will consume fewer saturated fats that are found in meats and dairy products. It is also a perfect way to get more phytochemicals, vitamin E and C, antioxidants, folate, potassium, magnesium, and fiber. Healthy levels of protein are also found in a plant-based diet.

Along with the added nutrients, a vegan diet will reduce your risk of several diseases. Eating more fruits and veggies will help with eye health and reducing the risk of macular degeneration and cataracts. The elimination of dairy also helps to improve arthritis symptoms. It will also reduce your risk of breast, colon, and prostate cancer, along with the reduction of blood pressure, cholesterol, and cardiovascular disease. There are just so many benefits you can get when going vegan. The good news is, you can get many of the health benefits without going all the way.

People in the modern society tend to eat too much of certain foods, causing a lot of problems. One, in particular, is animal proteins. For example, the average American will eat two times as much protein as they need for a healthy diet, which they get from red meat. According to The China Study, the animal protein actually promotes the growth of cancer. Your risk of ingesting Salmonella is also pretty much eliminated because it is contracted through raw chicken or eggs and can cause severe gastrointestinal illnesses.

Besides the obvious health benefits of following a vegan diet, it also plays an important part in promoting environmental sustainability. We can reduce the impact of climate change, rainforest destruction, and pollution just by becoming vegan.

A lot of people who follow a vegan diet do so out of concern for animals. Some of them are opposed to the animal's living conditions, while others view killing animals for food wrong.

Well, I assume that if you're reading this book, it means that you have already gone vegan or are currently considering to become one.

Eating plant-based doesn't mean just eating salads or boring rabbit food. The recipes in this book are delicious and heart-warming to the point where you will not want to give up the vegan diet.

In this book, you are going to learn the essential vegan staples, plant-based protein sources and 100 amazing vegan slow cooker recipes.

The recipes designed in this book are for people who, like me, love eating but don't want to spend too much time in the kitchen. If that sounds like you, keep reading and find out your favorite recipes to try out this week!

ESSENTIAL VEGAN STAPLES

Before we start cooking, it is important that you have a pantry stocked full of the foods that you need for a vegan diet. A well-stocked kitchen can make your life much easier.

The following are essentials that everybody needs to follow a plant-based diet.

Nuts

Besides the fact that they are great for heart health and giving you nutrients to live a long healthy life, nuts are also versatile and are needed for a vegan kitchen. You can toss them into a salad, use pine nuts to make pesto, and use cashews to make "cheese." You should also keep them in the freezer to extend their life.

Vegan Milk

To help you give up your dairy milk products, pick up some vegan milk products. This includes cashew, soy, rice, almond, hemp, and coconut milk. All of these provide you with lots of nutrients and fewer calories. Coconut milk is a great source of vitamin B and fiber, soy milk has lots of protein, and almond milk does not contain saturated fats or cholesterol.

Agave Nectar

Do you like to indulge in sweet foods from time to time, but you're looking for a healthier option? Agave nectar is a great substitute. This is sweeter than honey and comes from the agave plant. This is a great additive to your morning cup of coffee.

Herbs and Spices

To boost up the flavors in your meals, have herbs, and spices is a must. The following are some of the best:

- Turmeric: It adds an earthy flavor and color to your dishes. It also provides anti-inflammatory properties.
- Cayenne: If you like spicy foods, this is a great option.
- Cinnamon: This is perfect for sweet treats, but it is also perfect for savory dishes.
- Oregano: Essential for Italian dishes.
- Cumin: Perfect flavors for Mexican dishes and chilies.

Pasta

Pasta provides an important ingredient for many quick meals. Toss with some pasta sauce or some garlic and olive oil, and you have a meal in less than 20 minutes. Make sure you pick eggless and whole-grain.

Vegetable Stock

Add some veggies and vegetable stock, along with some seasonings to a pot, and you'll have yourself a tasty meal in a matter of minutes. This ingredient comes in handy with a lot of recipes like gravy and casserole.

Beans

Beans are packed full of protein, fiber, and antioxidants. Whether you used dried or canned, they are easily stored and add a little more heartiness to every meal. Bean juice can even double as a replacement for eggs.

Dates

This is a superfood for vegans. They are perfect as a binder for crusts. They also add a sweetness when added to smoothies and other baked goods. They are also full of beneficial nutrients like iron, calcium, and fiber.

Vegan Mayo

All traditional mayo contains eggs, but you can still have the creamy and rich flavor without the animal product. There are lots of vegan mayo options out there including Follow Your Heart's Vegenaise and Nayonaise.

Applesauce

Besides the fact that it is a tasty and wonderful treat on its own, applesauce also is a perfect substitute for oil, eggs, and butter. This makes it easy to make baked goods that delicious, moist, and best of all, vegan.

BEST PROTEIN SOURCES FOR VEGANS

While you are on a plant-based diet, it is important that you consume enough protein. Consuming protein promotes weight loss, muscle strength, and satiety. You will be surprised that consuming protein with a vegan diet is completely doable. There are some plants that have more protein than others.

Here are some of the best places to get protein sources for a plant-based diet.

Lentils

Lentils come in several varieties, but the most common are brown, green and red lentils. They are a great source of soluble fiber, protein, resistant starch, and complex carbohydrate.

Chia Seeds

"Chia" means strength in the language of the Mayans. The Mayans, Aztecs, and Incas have used these tiny seeds to boost energy. The number one reason is that they are rich in fiber, omega-3 fatty acids, protein, vitamins and minerals, all essential nutrients that most people are not getting enough of.

Quinoa

Quinoa looks similar to couscous, but it's much more nutritious. Apart from protein, it is full of fiber, iron, magnesium, and manganese. You can make Quinoa instead of rice, or mix it in salads or stews.

Chickpeas

Chickpeas, also known as garbanzo beans, offer a

range of health benefits. Like legumes, chickpeas are a form of complex carbohydrate that the body digests slowly and hence can help keep your blood sugar level stable. Chickpeas can also increase satiety, boost digestion, and increase protection against disease. Chickpeas are low in fat yet high in fiber and protein, which make you feel full for a longer period of time.

Edamame

Edamame has low calorie, contains no cholesterol and is a great source of protein, iron, and calcium. It is known as a complete protein because it contains all nine essential amino acids. It's thus similar in its protein content to animal-based protein sources, such as meat, dairy or eggs. To prepare Edamame, simply boil or steam them and then serve them with some salt. Try eating Edamame instead of high-calorie chips when you're craving some salty snacks.

Tempeh

Originated from Indonesia, Tempeh is a fermented food made from soybeans and is rich in protein, fiber, and healthy fat. 1 serving of tempeh contains around 20g protein. Although it's not as popular as tofu in the United States, it is actually less processed and offers more protein than tofu. Tempeh has mild, nutty flavor, and is easy to digest. Thus, you can replace chopped meat with tempeh in any recipe. You can also try adding some to a stir-fry instead of tofu or crumble into soups or meatless chili.

Goji berries

Goji berries, also known as wolfberries, are an excellent superfood. They have been used in traditional Chinese medicine for thousands of years. Goji berries have a mild tangy taste that is slightly sweet and sour. Goji berries are a great source of vitamins and minerals, including vitamin A, vitamin C, fiber, iron, zinc, and antioxidants. They are also an excellent protein source. 1 cup of goji berries contains up to 12 grams of protein. Add goji berries to your smoothie or your oatmeal, salad or soup.

Spirulina

Spirulina, a type of bacteria called cyanobacteria, is an organism that grows in both fresh and saltwater. It has the highest protein content, gram for gram, of any food on the planet. Just 2 tablespoons spirulina contains 8-gram protein. It tastes subtly sweet and nutty, but with a background seaweed flavor. Some people find it hard to enjoy its taste, however, the taste may vary, depending on the source of spirulina.

To make it more palatable, you can mix them with your smoothie or juice.

Nuts

Nuts are known as an excellent source of healthy, whole food fats. But you might not know that some of them are also a great source of protein. High protein nuts and seeds include pumpkin seeds, peanuts, pistachios, almonds, sunflower seeds, sesame seeds, and flax seeds. Their mix of omega-3 fatty acids, protein, and fiber will help you feel full and suppress your appetite. $^1/_4$ cup nuts contain around 7-9 gram protein.

VEGAN SLOW COOKER RECIPES

I

THE BASICS

HOMEMADE VEGETABLE BROTH

Serves: 10 cups

Prep Time: 15 minutes

Cook Time: 8 hours

Ingredients

- 1 large onion, chopped
- 2 garlic cloves, smashed
- 3 mushrooms, chopped
- 1 bell pepper, chopped
- 4 stalks celery, chopped
- 2 carrots, chopped
- 1 tbsp olive oil
- 1-2 tsp herbs of your choice. This can be thyme, rosemary, basil, or oregano.
- 10 cups water
- 2 tsp salt

Directions

1. Add garlic, onions, mushrooms, bell pepper, celery, carrots to your slow cooker.
2. Add olive oil and herbs. Give it a good stir.
3. Pour in water. Make sure everything is covered by the water.
4. Cover the cooker and cook on low for 8 hours.
5. When done, taste and add salt if needed.
6. Strain out the veggies and allow the broth to completely cool before freezing or refrigerating.

Nutrition Facts Per Serving

- Calories: 28 kcal
- Carbohydrates: 3.6g
- Dietary Fiber: 0.9g
- Protein: 0.65g
- Fat: 1.43g
- Saturated Fat: 0.2g

BASIC BEANS

Serves: 12

Prep Time: 10 minutes

Cook Time: 8 hours

Ingredients

- 1 lbs pinto beans
- 2 tbs salt
- 2 garlic cloves, smashed
- ½ onion, finely chopped
- ½ cup parsley, chopped (optional)

Directions

1. Pour beans into the slow cooker and cover with water. The water has to be enough to

cover the beans in your slow cooker for
about 1-2 inches.
2. Add garlic, onion, and salt.
3. Set the slow cooker for eight hours at a low
setting.
4. When done, add parsley. Stir well.
5. Enjoy.

Nutrition Facts Per Serving

- Calories: 135 kcal
- Carbohydrates: 24.4g
- Dietary Fiber: 6g
- Protein: 8.25g
- Fat: 0.49g
- Saturated Fat: 0.1g

EASY LENTILS

Serves: 4

Prep Time: 5 minutes

Cook Time: 3.5 hours

Ingredients

- 1 onion, diced
- 1 ½ cups green lentils, rinsed
- 2 small sweet potatoes, chunked
- 1 tsp ground cumin
- 3 cups homemade vegetable broth
- 2 cups fresh spinach

Directions

1. Place onion, lentils, sweet potatoes, broth, and cumin to the slow cooker.

2. Place the lid on the slow cooker. Set the temperature to high for three and a half hours. The lentils are done when they are tender.
3. Once the lentils are tender, add the spinach and stir again.
4. Add pepper and salt to taste.
5. Spoon into bowls and top with lime juice or a swirl of coconut milk.

Nutrition Facts Per Serving

- Calories: 141 kcal
- Carbohydrates: 26.9g
- Dietary Fiber: 4.4g
- Protein: 7.2g
- Fat: 1.93g
- Saturated Fat: 0.36g

MARINARA SAUCE

This is a very easy slow cooker marinara sauce. Try this sauce with pasta or vegan falafel. Your family is going to love it!

Serves: 6

Prep Time: 10 minutes

Cook Time: 8 hours

Ingredients

- 1 medium yellow onion, diced
- 4 cloves garlic, minced
- 2 (28 oz) cans diced tomatoes
- 1 (6 oz) can tomato paste
- ½ tbsp balsamic vinegar
- ½ tbsp dried oregano

- ½ tbsp dried basil
- 2 bay leaves
- Salt and pepper to taste

Directions

1. Add the onion and garlic to your cooker.
2. Next, add oregano, basil, bay leaves, balsamic vinegar, tomato paste, and diced tomatoes. Stir well.
3. Place the lid on the slow cooker. Set the temperature to low and cook for eight hours.
4. Taste and add pepper and salt if needed.
5. When cooled, you can either store it in the refrigerator or freeze it.

Nutrition Facts Per Serving

- Calories: 60 kcal
- Carbohydrates: 10.3g
- Dietary Fiber: 2.8g
- Protein: 2.21g
- Fat: 1.88g
- Saturated Fat: 0.26g

PERFECT WHITE RICE

Rice is a convenient and inexpensive staple in a vegan diet. You can choose any type of white rice for this recipe. I prefer Basmati rice or Jasmine rice, but you can choose whichever type you like.

Serves: 6

Prep Time: 5 minutes

Cook Time: 2-2.5 hours

Ingredients

- 2 cups white rice of choice, rinsed
- 4 cups water
- Pinch of salt

Directions

1. Place rice, salt, and water into your cooker.
2. Cook on low for two to two and a half hours, depending on your slow cooker.
3. Check to see if the liquid has been absorbed by the rice. The rice should be tender.
4. Fluff rice with a fork. Serve.

Nutrition Facts Per Serving

- Calories: 228 kcal
- Carbohydrates: 50g
- Dietary Fiber: 1.7g
- Protein: 4.2g
- Fat: 0.34g
- Saturated Fat: 0.1g

6

MASHED POTATOES

This is probably one of the easiest recipes you can make with a slow cooker. To make it taste even better, I use dairy free butter and vegetable broth to add some flavor but it is optional.

Serves: 6

Prep Time: 20 minutes

Cook Time: 2 hours

Ingredients

- 3 lbs potatoes, peeled and cut into chunks
- 24 oz homemade or low sodium vegetable broth
- 3 tbsp dairy free butter
- Salt and pepper to taste

Directions

1. Add the potatoes to your slow cooker.
2. Pour the broth and make sure that the potatoes are covered.
3. Cook on high for two hours. Check to see if the potatoes are tender.
4. Drain the potatoes over a bowl. Save the broth.
5. Add the potatoes back into the slow cooker. Add the dairy free butter and ¼ cup vegetable broth.
6. Mix with a hand mixer until smooth.
7. Add salt and pepper to taste. Serve.

Nutrition Facts Per Serving

- Calories: 261 kcal
- Carbohydrates: 56g
- Dietary Fiber: 7.5g
- Protein: 7.2g
- Fat: 1.3g
- Saturated Fat: 0.24g

CREAMY HUMMUS

I don't know about you, but I simply can't resist the creamy texture of hummus! This slow cooker version is super easy and I'm sure you will fall in love with it, too.

Serves: 4

Prep Time: 10 minutes

Cook Time: 4 hours

Ingredients

- 1 cup dried chickpeas
- 3 cups water
- 1 tsp salt
- 2 tbsp olive oil
- 1 tbsp fresh lemon juice

- 1 garlic clove, minced

Directions

1. Add the chickpeas, salt, and water to your slow cooker.
2. Cook on high for 4 hours, or until chickpeas are soft.
3. Drain the liquid from the chickpeas into a bowl and reserve the liquid.
4. Add the olive oil, lemon juice, garlic and 1/4 cup of reserved liquid to the food processor or blender. Blend for one minute.
5. Add the chickpeas and blend until creamy. Season to taste.
6. Top with olive oil and parsley. Enjoy!

Nutrition Facts Per Serving

- Calories: 251 kcal
- Carbohydrates: 32g
- Dietary Fiber: 6.1g
- Protein: 10.3g
- Fat: 9.78g
- Saturated Fat: 1.236g

8

CARAMELIZED ONIONS

Serves: 6

Prep Time: 15 minutes

Cook Time: 10 hours

Ingredients

- 5 lbs onions, thinly sliced
- 3 tbsp extra virgin olive oil
- ½ tsp salt

Directions

1. Add all of the onions to your cooker.
2. Add in the salt and the olive oil. Toss everything together.
3. Cover the cooker. Set the temperature to low for ten hours.

4. Stir onions every now and then to make sure they are cooking evenly.
5. After ten hours, the onions should be soft and golden. There will be some liquid in the bottom of the cooker. If you like the how your onions are now, stop the process here.
6. If you want your onions a deeper color and more concentrated, cook another four hours on low. This time leave the lid off just a bit so the liquid will be able to evaporate. Check each hour and stop when onions are to your liking.
7. Wait until completely cooled before putting in the freezer or refrigerator.

Nutrition Facts Per Serving

- Calories: 148 kcal
- Carbohydrates: 28.5g
- Dietary Fiber: 3.4g
- Protein: 3.05g
- Fat: 3.3g
- Saturated Fat: 0.4g

9

WINTER FRUIT COMPOTE

Who doesn't love some warm compote for dessert in the winter? You're going to love this compote because it's so fruity, sweet, simple and nutritious.

Serves: 12

Prep Time: 10 minutes

Cook Time: 5 hours

Ingredients

- 2 small apples, peeled and sliced
- 4 fresh peaches, sliced
- ½ cup dried cranberries
- ½ cup dried apricots
- 3/4 cup fresh orange juice
- 1 tsp ground cinnamon

- ¼ tsp ground ginger
- 4 tbsp brown sugar

Directions

1. In the slow cooker, add the apples, peaches, cranberries, and apricots.
2. Add orange juice, ginger, cinnamon, and sugar.
3. Cover and cook on low for 5 hours.
4. Serve warm over vegan pancakes, waffles, or vegan ice cream.

Nutrition Facts Per Serving

- Calories: 115 kcal
- Carbohydrates: 29.6g
- Dietary Fiber: 2.2g
- Protein: 0.84g
- Fat: 0.29g
- Saturated Fat: 0.02g

II

BREAKFAST

CRANBERRY ALMOND QUINOA

It is important that we consume something healthy first thing in the morning. This recipe is full of nutritious and delicious ingredients that will bring you energy for the entire day.

Serves: 4

Prep Time: 5 minutes

Cook Time: 2 hours

Ingredients

- ½ cup dried cranberries
- 1 cup uncooked quinoa
- 1/8 cup almonds, chopped
- 1/8 cup coconut flakes
- 3 cup coconut water

- 1 tsp vanilla extract
- 4 tsp maple syrup

Directions

1. Place all ingredients in your slow cooker.
2. Cover and cook on high for two hours.
3. When done, stir to combine.
4. Serve.

Nutrition Facts Per Serving

- Calories: 293 kcal
- Carbohydrates: 52.3g
- Dietary Fiber: 6.7g
- Protein: 8.4g
- Fat: 6.3g
- Saturated Fat: 1.5g

BAKED APPLES

Serves: 5

Prep Time: 10 minutes

Cook Time: 2 hours

Ingredients

- 5 tsp maple syrup
- 5 medium apples
- 1 cup granola
- Non-dairy whipped cream or vegan ice cream (optional)

Directions

1. Cut the top off and use a melon baller to scoop out the core of each apple. Do not remove the bottom.

2. Stuff the granola into the cavity of each apple.
3. Put the apples in the slow cooker.
4. Add one teaspoon maple syrup to every apple.
5. Cover and cook on high for two hours.
6. Serve with non-dairy whipped cream or vegan ice cream.

Nutrition Facts Per Serving

- Calories: 131 kcal
- Carbohydrates: 32.2g
- Dietary Fiber: 4.6g
- Protein: 0.9g
- Fat: 1.14g
- Saturated Fat: 0.15g

BREAKFAST BURRITOS

This recipe is perfect for that run in the morning breakfast. Simply set the slow cooker the night before and then wrap the fillings with the tortillas the next day in the morning.

Serves: 8

Prep Time: 15 minutes

Cook Time: 6 hours

Ingredients

- 8 whole wheat tortillas
- 1 (15 oz) can black beans, rinsed
- ¼ cup scallions, chopped
- 1 green pepper, finely chopped
- 1 tomato, diced

- ½ cup water
- 1 cup salsa
- ½ tsp paprika
- ½ tsp ground turmeric
- ¼ tsp chili powder
- ¼ tsp ground cumin
- Salt and pepper to taste

Directions

1. Put the black beans in the bottom of a slow cooker.
2. Add paprika, turmeric, chili powder, cumin, water, salsa, green pepper, and scallions. Add pepper and salt.
3. Cover and cook on low for six hours.
4. Serve with warm tortillas and fresh diced tomato.

Nutrition Facts Per Serving

- Calories: 325 kcal
- Carbohydrates: 55.79g
- Dietary Fiber: 13.3g
- Protein: 16.35g
- Fat: 4.9g
- Saturated Fat: 2.2g

13

CHAI APPLESAUCE

Serves: 5

Prep Time: 20 minutes

Cook Time: 7 hours

Ingredients

- 8 medium apples, peeled, cored and cut into chunks
- 1 stick cinnamon
- 1 tsp lemon juice
- 1 tsp vanilla extract
- 5 tsp brown sugar
- ½ tsp ground ginger
- ½ tsp ground cardamom
- ½ tsp ground nutmeg
- ½ tsp ground cloves

Directions

1. Add everything to your slow cooker. Stir well to combine.
2. Cook on low for seven hours.
3. Remove cinnamon stick.
4. Take out half of the apple chunks and place them in a large bowl.
5. With an immersion blender, mix the rest of the fruit until smooth. Add the reserved apple chunks back into the slow cooker.
6. Serve.

Nutrition Facts Per Serving

- Calories: 174 kcal
- Carbohydrates: 45.3g
- Dietary Fiber: 7.1g
- Protein: 0.82g
- Fat: 0.6g
- Saturated Fat: 0.15g

14

CHOCOLATE CHERRY OATMEAL

This is the perfect solution if you are craving choco-late for breakfast. Start your day with a deliciously comforting bowl!

Serves: 4

Prep Time: 10 minutes

Cook Time: 8 hours

Ingredients

- 1 cup steel cut oats
- 2 cup water
- 2 tbsp unsweetened cocoa powder (make sure it's vegan)
- 2 cup unsweetened vanilla almond milk
- ¼ cup maple syrup

- ⅓ cup dried tart cherries

Directions

1. Add all of the above into your cooker.
2. Cover and cook on low for eight hours. When finished, set the slow cooker on warm.
3. Top with cherry, berries, bananas, and nuts. Enjoy!

Nutrition Facts Per Serving

- Calories: 262 kcal
- Carbohydrates: 50.3g
- Dietary Fiber: 5.6g
- Protein: 7.74g
- Fat: 4.3g
- Saturated Fat: 0.69g

15

PUMPKIN OATMEAL

Serves: 4

Prep Time: 5 minutes

Cook Time: 8 hours

Ingredients

- ½ cup steel cut oats
- ½ cup pumpkin, pureed
- 1 tsp pumpkin pie spice
- 1 ½ cup water
- ¼ cup pecans, chopped
- 3 tbsp brown sugar

Directions

1. Mix pumpkin pie spice, brown sugar,

pumpkin puree, and 1 ½ cups water in a bowl.

2. Add the oats to a large 23 oz oven-safe bowl. Pour pumpkin mix on top. Stir.

3. Carefully place the bowl in the middle of the crockpot. Add water to crock pot until it reaches about one inch below the top of the bowl. Sprinkle pecans on top.

4. Cover and cook on low for eight hours.

5. In the morning, turn off slow cooker. Take off the lid and let bowl cool a bit so you can lift it out without getting burned.

6. When cool enough, remove the bowl and stir everything well.

7. Top with brown sugar and more pecans if desired.

Nutrition Facts Per Serving

- Calories: 161 kcal
- Carbohydrates: 24.6g
- Dietary Fiber: 3.1g
- Protein: 4.12g
- Fat: 5.8g
- Saturated Fat: 0.6g

16

MAPLE PEAR OATMEAL

Serves: 3

Prep Time: 5 minutes

Cook Time: 8 hours

Ingredients

- 1 pear, sliced
- ½ cup steel cut oats
- ½ tsp maple extract
- ½ tsp vanilla extract
- 2 cups unsweetened coconut milk
- 1 cup water

Directions

1. Add all ingredients to the slow cooker. Stir.
2. Cover and cook on low for eight hours.

3. Serve with some cinnamon, nutmeg, or walnuts.

Nutrition Facts Per Serving

- Calories: 268 kcal
- Carbohydrates: 14.8g
- Dietary Fiber: 2.9g
- Protein: 4.47g
- Fat: 25g
- Saturated Fat: 21.5g

17

BLUEBERRY OATMEAL

Blueberries are an antioxidant superfood. They can lower your risk of heart disease and cancer. Add these to your morning oatmeal and enjoy a beautiful morning!

Serves: 4

Prep Time: 5 minutes

Cook Time: 8 hours

Ingredients

- 1 cup steel cut oats
- 1 cup frozen blueberries
- ¾ cup coconut milk
- ½ tbsp vanilla extract
- 2 tbsp light agave

Directions

1. Coat your slow cooker with nonstick spray.
2. Add frozen blueberries, ¼ cup coconut milk, and oats in the slow cooker. Stir.
3. Cover and cook on low for eight hours.
4. Add agave, vanilla extract, and ½ cup coconut milk.
5. Serve with coconut flakes and fresh blueberries. Enjoy!

Nutrition Facts Per Serving

- Calories: 285 kcal
- Carbohydrates: 34.5g
- Dietary Fiber: 6.7g
- Protein: 7.8g
- Fat: 13.7g
- Saturated Fat: 10g

APPLE PIE OATMEAL

Serves: 4

Prep Time: 10 minutes

Cook Time: 4 hours

Ingredients

- 1 cup steel cut oats
- 1 ½ cup almond milk
- 1 ½ cup water
- 2 tsp vanilla extract
- ¼ tsp ground nutmeg
- 1 tbsp ground flax seed
- ½ tsp ground cinnamon
- ¼ tsp ground ginger

Directions

1. Coat your slow cooker with nonstick spray.
2. Peel, core, and slice apples. Add the apples to the slow cooker.
3. Add oats, ground flax seed, ginger, nutmeg, cinnamon, vanilla, 1 ½ cup water, and 1 ½ cup almond milk to the slow cooker and stir.
4. Cover and cook for four hours on high.
5. Remove the lid and stir again to make sure everything is well combined.
6. Top with more apples, cinnamon, or walnuts.

Nutrition Facts Per Serving

- Calories: 215 kcal
- Carbohydrates: 33.5g
- Dietary Fiber: 5.1g
- Protein: 7.7g
- Fat: 5.5g
- Saturated Fat: 0.8g

19

BANANA NUT OATMEAL

Serves: 4

Prep Time: 5 minutes

Cook Time: 8 hours

Ingredients

- 1 cup steel cut oats
- 1 ripe banana, chopped
- ¼ cup walnuts, chopped
- 2 cups almond milk
- 2 cups water
- 1 tsp vanilla extract
- 2 tsp cinnamon
- 2 tbsp flaxseed meal
- ½ tsp nutmeg
- ½ tsp salt

Directions

1. Add everything to your cooker and mix.
2. Cover and cook on low for eight hours.
3. In the morning, open the lid and stir.
4. Top with fresh banana slices, brown sugar, or more walnuts. Enjoy!

Nutrition Facts Per Serving

- Calories: 291 kcal
- Carbohydrates: 44g
- Dietary Fiber: 7.9g
- Protein: 9.2g
- Fat: 9.5g
- Saturated Fat: 1.1g

20

CARROT CAKE OATMEAL

Do you love carrot cake? Take the flavors of carrot cake and make an incredibly delicious and healthy breakfast bowl!

Serves: 3

Prep Time: 5 minutes

Cook Time: 8 hours

Ingredients

- ½ cup steel cut oats
- 1 carrot, grated
- 1 cup coconut milk
- 1 cup water
- 2 tbsp walnuts, chopped
- 1 tsp ground cinnamon

- 2 tbsp brown sugar
- ½ tsp of salt

Directions

1. Coat your cooker with nonstick spray.
2. Add carrots, coconut milk, oats, brown sugar, cinnamon, and salt. Stir.
3. Cover and cook on low for eight hours.
4. In the morning, remove the lid and stir to combine everything.
5. Sprinkle with more brown sugar, if you like, and top with the walnuts.

Nutrition Facts Per Serving

- Calories: 363 kcal
- Carbohydrates: 33.8g
- Dietary Fiber: 5.9g
- Protein: 7.7g
- Fat: 24g
- Saturated Fat: 17.4g

21

ALMOND BUTTER OATMEAL

Serves: 4

Prep Time: 5 minutes

Cook Time: 8 hours

Ingredients

- 1 cup steel cut oats
- 4 tbsp almond butter
- 1 cup almond milk
- 1 cup water
- 1 tsp vanilla extract
- 2 tbsp brown sugar
- Pinch of salt

Directions

1. In a 4-cup glass measuring jug, add the

water, almond milk, oats, vanilla, and salt. Stir well.
2. Place in your slow cooker and add enough water to the cooker so that it reaches halfway up the side of the jug.
3. Cover and cook on low for eight hours.
4. Stir in the almond butter and brown sugar.
5. Serve.

Nutrition Facts Per Serving

- Calories: 315 kcal
- Carbohydrates: 43.3g
- Dietary Fiber: 6g
- Protein: 10.4g
- Fat: 12.3g
- Saturated Fat: 1.5g

III

BREAD

22

HERB AND SEED MONKEY BREAD

Serves: 12

Prep Time: 1 hour

Cook Time: 2 hours

Ingredients

- 1 tsp salt
- 2 tbsp chia seeds
- 1 tbsp olive oil
- 2 tbsp chopped parsley
- 2 tbsp flaked almonds
- 1 ½ to 2 cups all-purpose flour
- 1 packet active dry yeast
- 1 ½ tbsp sugar
- 1 cup lukewarm water
- 2 tbsp sesame seeds

Directions

1. Prepare slow cooker by spraying with cooking spray and lining with parchment paper. Make sure parchment paper is hanging out so you can lift it out when done. Spray parchment paper with cooking spray, too.
2. Mix yeast, sugar, and water in a bowl and let sit for five minutes until water bubbles.
3. Add salt, flour, and olive oil to yeast. Mix until dough forms. Begin with the lowest amount of flour and add until your dough isn't sticky.
4. Knead for ten minutes. Sit into an oiled bowl and top with a kitchen towel. Allow it to rest for an hour in a warm spot.
5. When the hour is up, punch out all the air and roll into golf ball sized balls. Slightly dampen each ball with your fingers and roll each one into a different topping. Place into the prepared slow cooker.
6. Let sit for 30 minutes before cooking.
7. Cover the cooker. Set to high for 1 to 2 ½ hours. Check for doneness after one hour.
8. When done, let cook for about 20 minutes before carefully removing and flipping onto a wire rack to completely cool.
9. Eat immediately.

Nutrition Facts Per Serving

- Calories: 94 kcal
- Carbohydrates: 14.4g
- Dietary Fiber: 1.6g
- Protein: 2.58g
- Fat: 2.97g
- Saturated Fat: 0.39g

23

WHOLE WHEAT NO KNEAD BREAD

Serves: varies

Prep Time: 1 hour

Cook Time: 2 hours

Ingredients

- 1 tbsp rolled oats
- 4 cups whole wheat flour
- 2 ¼ tsp active dry yeast
- 2 cups warm water
- 1 ½ tsp kosher salt
- Coarse salt

Directions

1. Whisk the yeast, salt, and flour together.

Add in the water and stir with wooden spoon until thoroughly combined. This dough will be sticky.

2. Cover with saran wrap. Keep in a warm spot for one hour.
3. Grease the slow cooker with olive oil.
4. Sprinkle top of dough with some flour and work the dough out of the bowl and put it into the slow cooker. Shape into a circle with the wooden spoon.
5. Place a towel over it and let it sit for 30 minutes.
6. Brush top of dough with 2 tsp olive oil, score the top with an X and sprinkle the coarse salt and oats on top.
7. Place lid on slow cooker. Set on high for one to two and a half hours. Check for doneness after one hour.
8. Bread will be done when deep golden brown.

Nutrition Facts Per Serving

- Calories: 138 kcal
- Carbohydrates: 29.1g
- Dietary Fiber: 4.5g

- Protein: 5.59g
- Fat: 1.06g
- Saturated Fat: 0.146g

24

WHOLE WHEAT STOUT BREAD

Serves: varies

Prep Time: 1 hour

Cook Time: 2 hours

Ingredients

- 3 tbsp brown sugar
- 1 can full-fat coconut milk
- ½ tsp almond extract
- 2 tsp olive oil
- 3 cups flour, whole wheat
- 1 cup stout beer
- 1 packet rapid rise yeast

Directions

1. Fit a stand mixer with a dough hook. Place

yeast, brown sugar, and flour. Stir to combine.

2. Open can of coconut milk. Scrape out one-half c of coconut fat from the top.

3. Put the coconut fat and beer in a microwavable bowl. Heat in one-minute increments until temperature reaches 125 degrees.

4. Add almond extract, and oil to beer mixture. Stir to combine. Pour into flour.

5. Start the mixer on low and soon go to high. Beat until dough stays around the hook and isn't sticky. This will take about six minutes.

6. Place the dough into a bowl that has been oiled. Place a towel over the dough and let it rise until it has doubled. This will take about 60 minutes.

7. Place the dough on a surface that has been floured lightly and knead for about three minutes.

8. Shape loaf into a circle. Put in bottom of slow cooker. Cover with lid. Let rise for another 20 minutes.

9. Set on low for two hours. Check for doneness after one hour.

10. When done, bread will be dark brown.

Nutrition Facts Per Serving

- Calories: 192 kcal
- Carbohydrates: 25.65g
- Dietary Fiber: 3.4g
- Protein: 5.91g
- Fat: 8.35g
- Saturated Fat: 5.721g

25

FOCACCIA BREAD

Serves: 20

Prep Time: 02:05

Cook Time: 2 hours

Ingredients

- 2 tsp salt
- 4 cups bread flour
- 1 tsp sugar
- 1 ½ cups warm water
- 2 tbsp oil
- 1 package active dry yeast

Directions

1. Put yeast into the water for ten minutes.

2. Combine salt, sugar, oil, and flour in a stand mixer. Add yeast.
3. Beat using a paddle attachment until dough comes together.
4. Switch to a dough hook and beat unto dough is elastic and smooth.
5. Grease a bowl with oil and add to the dough. Coat the dough with the oil. Cover with kitchen towel and put in a warm spot into dough doubles. This will take about one hour.
6. Punch air out of dough. Place back into bowl and cover. Allow to rise one more time about 40 minutes.
7. Coat bottom of slow cooker with olive oil. Sprinkle with sea salt. If you want to add herbs to top of bread, do so now.
8. Put dough in the slow cooker and spread out slightly. Cover the cooker and let sit for 25 more minutes. Press fingers into the dough to make small indentations. Set the temperature to low for two hours. Check for doneness after one hour.
9. Cook until golden brown and crusty.
10. Trim the edges and cut in half. Cut each half into one-inch pieces. You should get about 20 pieces.

Nutrition Facts Per Serving

- Calories: 54 kcal
- Carbohydrates: 6.22g
- Dietary Fiber: .5g
- Protein: 1.28g
- Fat: 2.68g
- Saturated Fat: 0.4g

IV

SNACKS & APPETIZERS

VEGAN SEITAN CARNITAS

Carnitas is traditionally made with pork and is a well-known Mexican comfort food. You will love this vegan, seitan version! You can generally find seitan in the refrigerator section of health food stores.

Serves: 8

Prep Time: 15 minutes

Cook Time: 5 hours

Ingredients

- 2 (8 oz) packages scitan, drained
- 8 corn tortillas
- 1 cup vegetable broth, divided
- 1 clove garlic, minced

- ½ cup cilantro, chopped
- Juice of one lime
- 1 tsp cumin
- 1 tsp oregano
- ½ tsp salt
- Optional toppings: guacamole and tomatoes

Directions

1. In a skillet over medium-high heat, brown seitan for about five minutes.
2. Add ¼ cup vegetable broth to the skillet and cook for another 2-3 minutes.
3. Add the mixture to the slow cooker.
4. Add the rest of the vegetable broth, lime juice, garlic, cumin, oregano, cilantro, and salt to the cooker. Stir it all together.
5. Cover and cook on low for five hours.
6. Serve with warm tortillas and top with seitan carnitas and other desired toppings.

Nutrition Facts Per Serving

- Calories: 137 kcal
- Carbohydrates: 14.6g
- Dietary Fiber: 1.7g

- Protein: 15.5g
- Fat: 2 g
- Saturated Fat: 0.1g

RAINBOW PANZANELLA SALAD

Color, flavor, nutrients; you name it, this salad has it. What's even better, your kids will love it. Brighten up your dinner table with this delicious rainbow Panzanella salad!

Serves: 4

Prep Time: 10 minutes

Cook Time: 6 hours

Ingredients

For the salad:

- 3 cups purple potatoes, cut into chunks
- 2 cups golden beets, cut into chunks
- 3 cups tomatoes, chopped (you can use

different types of tomatoes to make the salad more colorful)

- 2 cups water

For the dressing:

- ¼ cup olive oil
- 1 tsp Dijon mustard
- 3 tbsp balsamic vinegar
- ¼ cup basil, chopped
- 1 tsp fresh thyme leaves, chopped
- 1 cup bread cubes

Directions

1. Add beets, potatoes, and water into the slow cooker.
2. Cook on low for six hours. Potatoes and beets should be tender.
3. When done, drain them using a colander and rinse with cold water.
4. Mix dressing ingredients in a small bowl.
5. Place beets, potatoes, and tomatoes into a large mixing bowl.
6. Add the dressing and mix well to combine everything.
7. Add bread cubes just before serving.

Nutrition Facts Per Serving

- Calories: 335 kcal
- Carbohydrates: 49g
- Dietary Fiber: 7.1g
- Protein: 5.9g
- Fat: 14.2g
- Saturated Fat: 2.03g

GREAT NORTHERN BEAN AND ALMOND DIP

This is a gluten-free, oil-free dip recipe with a nutty, dense flavor. You can serve it with veggies, tofu, tempeh or toasted bread cubes.

Serves: 4

Prep Time: 10 minutes

Cook Time: 8 hours

Ingredients

- 1 cup slivered almonds
- ½ cup great northern beans, dried
- 2 cup water
- 1½ tsp nutritional yeast flakes
- ¼ tsp pepper
- ½ tsp salt

Directions

1. Add almonds, great northern beans, and water in the slow cooker.
2. Cover and cook on high for eight hours.
3. When done, carefully pour into the blender. Add pepper, salt, and yeast. Blend until smooth.
4. Serve.

Nutrition Facts Per Serving

- Calories: 288 kcal
- Carbohydrates: 22.5g
- Dietary Fiber: 9.2g
- Protein: 13g
- Fat: 18g
- Saturated Fat: 1.4g

29

VEGAN CHILI QUESO DIP

Cooking this queso in the slow cooker is super easy and it helps to meld all of the flavors together. Just 10-minute prep and the slow cooker will handle the rest!

Serves: 6

Prep Time: 10 minutes

Cook Time: 6 hours

Ingredients

- 3 cups cauliflower florets
- 1 medium carrot, sliced
- ½ cup raw cashews
- 2 cups water

- ½ cup nutritional yeast
- ¼ tsp Dijon mustard
- ½ tsp chili powder
- 1 tsp paprika
- ½ cup tomato, diced
- ¼ cup red onions, finely chopped
- 1 tbsp green chilies, finely chopped
- ¼ cup cilantro, minced

Directions

1. Add the cauliflower, cashews, carrots, and 2 cups water to the slow cooker.
2. Cover and cook on low for six hours.
3. Add the cooked mixture to a blender with Dijon mustard, chili powder, paprika, and nutritional yeast. Add some water if needed.
4. Stir in the tomatoes, red onions, green chilies, and cilantro.
5. Serve warm.

Nutrition Facts Per Serving

- Calories: 120 kcal
- Carbohydrates: 11.9g

- Dietary Fiber: 3.5g
- Protein: 8.9g
- Fat: 4.9g
- Saturated Fat: 0.87g

30

WHITE BEAN QUESO DIP

Serves: 8

Prep Time: 5 minutes

Cook Time: 2 hours

Ingredients

- 1 15 oz can white beans
- ½ cup unsweetened almond milk
- ¼ cup nutritional yeast
- ½ cup raw cashews
- 1 tbsp green chilies
- 1 tsp chili powder
- 1 tsp paprika
- ½ tsp garlic powder
- 1 tsp salt

Directions

1. Add everything to your food processor and mix until creamy. If it is too thick, add more almond milk.
2. Cover and cook on low for 2 hours; stir occasionally.
3. When done, switch to warm setting until ready to eat.

Nutrition Facts Per Serving

- Calories: 229 kcal
- Carbohydrates: 38.7g
- Dietary Fiber: 9.6g
- Protein: 16.07g
- Fat: 1.94g
- Saturated Fat: 0.33g

POTATOES AU GRATIN

These creamy potatoes au gratin are always welcome at the dinner table, and they're really simple to make. It is a side dish that your entire family will love!

Serves: 4

Prep Time: 5 minutes

Cook Time: 8 hours

Ingredients

- 4 medium potatoes, peeled and sliced
- 1 cup carrots, peeled, sliced and cooked
- 2 cups cauliflower florets, cooked
- 1 cup unsweetened almond milk
- ½ cup nutritional yeast

- ½ tsp paprika
- ½ tsp salt
- ½ tsp pepper

Directions

1. Add the carrots, cauliflower florets, almond milk, yeast, paprika, salt and pepper in a blender. Blend until smooth.
2. Pour ⅓ of the mixture in the slow cooker. Layer with ⅓ of the potatoes. Repeat this process until all ingredients are used up.
3. Cover and cook on low for eight hours.
4. Serve.

Nutrition Facts Per Serving

- Calories: 405 kcal
- Carbohydrates: 82.47g
- Dietary Fiber: 14g
- Protein: 18.16g
- Fat: 1.59g
- Saturated Fat: 0.14g

EGGPLANT AND OLIVE TAPENADE

The word "tapenade" actually comes from tapeno, which is the Provençal word for capers. It consists of puréed or finely chopped olives, capers, and olive oil. If you love these ingredients, you are sure to love this recipe with eggplant!

Serves: 4

Prep Time: 15 minutes

Cook Time: 8 hours

Ingredients

- 3 medium eggplant, chopped
- ½ cups tomatoes, diced
- 1 (6 oz) can green olives, pitted and chopped

- 3 cloves garlic, minced
- 2 tsp capers
- 2 tsp balsamic vinegar
- 1 tsp dried basil

Directions

1. Add eggplant, tomatoes, garlic, capers, and olives to the slow cooker.
2. Cover and cook on low for eight hours.
3. Just before serving, add vinegar, basil, salt, and pepper.
4. Serve with your favorite bread or crackers.

Nutrition Facts Per Serving

- Calories: 149 kcal
- Carbohydrates: 27.4g
- Dietary Fiber: 13.5g
- Protein: 4.7g
- Fat: 4.6g
- Saturated Fat: 0.66g

33

VEGAN PIMENTO CHEESE FONDUE

Serves: 10

Prep Time: 5 minutes

Cook Time: 2 hours

Ingredients

- 1 (15 oz) can white beans, drained
- ½ tsp stone ground mustard
- 2 cups vegan cheddar cheese
- 1 jar diced pimentos, drained
- 2 tbsp vegan bouillon
- 2 tbsp olive oil
- ¾ cup water

Directions

1. Add water and beans in a food processor and mix until creamy.
2. Grease your cooker. Add puree and the rest of the ingredients to the slow cooker.
3. Cover and cook on low for one and a half hours.
4. Stir every 20 minutes. If you want the fondue thinner, add more water.

Nutrition Facts Per Serving

- Calories: 168 kcal
- Carbohydrates: 15.54g
- Dietary Fiber: 2.4g
- Protein: 10.19g
- Fat: 7.54g
- Saturated Fat: 3.3g

34

VEGAN "CHEESY" CAULIFLOWER DIP

Serves: 4

Prep Time: 10 minutes

Cook Time: 4 hours

Ingredients

- 1 large head cauliflower, cut into florets
- 2 cloves garlic, minced
- ½ cup unsweetened almond milk
- 1 cup water
- ½ tbsp lemon juice
- ¼ cup nutritional yeast
- ¼ tsp dry mustard (or ¼ tbsp of prepared mustard)
- ¼ tsp paprika
- ½ tsp salt

Directions

1. Add cauliflower florets, garlic, mustard, paprika and almond milk to the slow cooker.
2. Cover and cook on high for 2 hours. The cauliflower should be tender when it is done. Wait until the cooked content is cool before blending.
3. When the cooked content is cool, transfer it to your blender. Add the water, lemon juice, nutritional yeast, and salt in the blender. Blend until smooth.
4. Pour the sauce back into the slow cooker and cook on low for 1-2 hours or until desired thickness.

Nutrition Facts Per Serving

- Calories: 100 kcal
- Carbohydrates: 16.85g
- Dietary Fiber: 5.6g
- Protein: 8.6g
- Fat: 1.1g
- Saturated Fat: .036g

35

VEGAN MAC AND CHEESE

Who doesn't love a good, creamy Mac and Cheese? What's better, even if you are vegan, you can enjoy this dairy-free version. You won't believe how delicious dairy-free mac and cheese can be!

Serves: 4

Prep Time: 10 minutes

Cook Time: 2 hours

Ingredients

- 1 ½ cups uncooked gluten-free macaroni
- ½ cup raw cashews, soaked in water for 2 hours and drained
- 2 cloves minced garlic
- 2 tbsp lemon juice

- 3 cups water
- ¼ cup nutritional yeast
- 2 tsp sea salt

Directions

1. In a blender, add the cashews, 2 cups of water, nutritional yeast, garlic, salt and lemon juice. Blend until smooth.
2. Add the macaroni to your slow cooker, and pour the sauce over the top. Add another cup of water.
3. Cover and cook on high for two hours. Check to see if the pasta is cooked to your preference.
4. When done, stir well to make sure everything is well incorporated.
5. Taste and add pepper and salt if needed.

Nutrition Facts Per Serving

- Calories: 418 kcal
- Carbohydrates: 46.9g
- Dietary Fiber: 3.9g
- Protein: 17.3g
- Fat: 19.42g
- Saturated Fat: 3.4g

REFRIED BEANS

Serves: 2

Prep Time: 5 minutes

Cook Time: 4 hours

Ingredients

- 1 (15 oz) can pinto beans, rinsed
- 1 small yellow onion, finely diced
- 1 clove garlic, minced
- 1 tsp coconut oil
- 5 cups water
- 2 cups vegetable broth
- 1 tbsp jalapeno, minced
- 1 tsp chili powder
- 1 tsp cumin
- 1 ½ tsp sea salt
- 1 tsp pepper

Directions

1. Place all the ingredients in a large slow cooker.
2. Cover and cook on high for four hours.
3. When done, place a colander over a stock pot and drain as much water as you can from the beans.
4. Use a potato masher or an immersion blender to mash the beans into a desired texture. Use some of the reserved liquid to help thin.
5. Serve. Add salt and pepper if needed.

Nutrition Facts Per Serving

- Calories: 350 kcal
- Carbohydrates: 53.8g
- Dietary Fiber: 13.4g
- Protein: 16.2g
- Fat: 9.3g
- Saturated Fat: 2.9g

V

SOUPS, STEWS & CHILI

37

VEGGIE CHILI WITH SUMMER SQUASH

Serves: 8

Prep Time: 15 minutes

Cook Time: 8 hours

Ingredients

- 1 medium yellow onion, diced
- 2 summer squash, chopped
- 1 (15 oz) can kidney beans, rinsed and drained
- 1 (15 oz) can black beans, rinsed and drained
- 1 (15 oz) can organic whole corn, drained
- 1 16 oz) can sliced mushrooms
- 1 (15-oz) can tomato sauce
- ½ cups water
- 1 ½ cups vegetable stock

- 1 tsp chili powder
- 1 tsp ground cumin
- Salt and pepper to taste
- Diced avocado, for serving (optional)

Directions

1. Place all of the ingredients in your cooker. Stir well. Season with a bit of pepper and salt.
2. Cook on low for eight hours. Serve with diced avocado if you like.

Nutrition Facts Per Serving

- Calories: 218 kcal
- Carbohydrates: 39.8 g
- Dietary Fiber: 10.5 g
- Protein: 9.87g
- Fat: 3 g
- Saturated Fat: 0.86 g

38

LENTIL CHILI

Lentils are a very important source of protein for vegans. With a mix of spices, sweet potatoes and carrots, this recipe will warm you up during the cold winter months!

Serves: 6

Prep Time: 10 minutes

Cook Time: 7 hours

Ingredients

- 1 (16 oz) can brown lentils, rinsed
- 1 medium onion, diced
- 2 cloves garlic, minced
- 2 small carrots, diced
- 1 small sweet potato, cut into small cubes

- 3 cups vegetable broth
- ¼ cup tomato paste
- 1 tsp cumin
- 2 tbsp chili powder
- 1 tsp paprika
- Salt and black pepper to taste
- Optional toppings: chopped cilantro and avocado

Directions

1. Place all ingredients except the cilantro in your slow cooker. Stir well to combine.
2. Cover and cook on low for 7 hours. Season once done.
3. Serve topped with cilantro and avocado.

Nutrition Facts Per Serving

- Calories: 133 kcal
- Carbohydrates: 28.4 g
- Dietary Fiber: 3.9 g
- Protein: 8.5 g
- Fat: 1.07 g
- Saturated Fat: 0.15 g

39

VEGETABLE CHILI

Serves: 6

Prep Time: 10 minutes

Cook Time: 6 hours

Ingredients

- 4 garlic cloves, minced
- 1 white onion, diced
- 3 (15 oz) cans red kidney beans, rinsed
- 2 (14 oz) cans diced tomatoes
- 1 cup farro
- 4 cups vegetable broth
- 2 tbsp chili powder
- 1 tsp brown sugar

Directions

1. Combine everything in your cooker.
2. Set the cooker to low and cook for six hours.
3. Taste and adjust any seasonings.

Nutrition Facts Per Serving

- Calories: 283 kcal
- Carbohydrates: 54.78 g
- Dietary Fiber: 16 g
- Protein: 15.11 g
- Fat: 2.12 g
- Saturated Fat: 0.49 g

40

ASIAN CABBAGE SOUP

This warming and healing Asian soup is so easy to make, and it would make a perfect light dinner when you simply want to consume lots of veggies.

Serves: 4

Prep Time: 10 minutes

Cook Time: 6 hours

Ingredients

- ½ head of cabbage, chopped
- ½ onion, sliced thinly
- 2 cloves garlic, minced
- 3 tsp minced ginger
- 1 (15 oz) can organic whole corn, drained
- 1 stalk celery, sliced

- 4 cups vegetable broth
- 2 cups water
- 1 tsp sesame oil
- 1 tbsp soy sauce
- Salt to taste

Directions

1. Place all ingredients in your slow cooker except the soy sauce and the sesame oil. Stir well to combine.
2. Cover and cook on low for 6 hours.
3. Add sesame oil and soy sauce and then serve.

Nutrition Facts Per Serving

- Calories: 128 kcal
- Carbohydrates: 25.6 g
- Dietary Fiber: 8.6 g
- Protein: 3.7 g
- Fat: 2.9 g
- Saturated Fat: 0.4 g

41

WHITE BEAN SOUP

Serves: 6

Prep Time: 10 minutes

Cook Time: 8 hours

Ingredients

- 1½ cups dry cannellini beans, rinsed
- 2 tbsp olive oil
- 2 stalks celery, sliced
- 2 small carrots, diced
- 1 medium yellow onion, diced
- 8 cups vegetable broth
- ½ tsp rosemary
- ½ tsp thyme
- 1 bay leaf
- Salt and black pepper to taste

Directions

1. Add everything to your cooker and add some pepper and salt. Stir everything well.
2. Cover and cook on low for eight hours.
3. Serve.

Nutrition Facts Per Serving

- Calories: 241 kcal
- Carbohydrates: 36.2 g
- Dietary Fiber: 10.2 g
- Protein: 10.5 g
- Fat: 6.7 g
- Saturated Fat: 1 g

42

FARRO SPLIT PEA SOUP

Serves: 6

Prep Time: 5 minutes

Cook Time: 8 hours

Ingredients

- 2 cups turnip
- 1 ½ cup farro
- 1 cup split peas
- 8 cups water
- 2 tsp garam masala
- 2 tsp paprika
- 1 tsp turmeric
- Salt and pepper to taste

Directions

1. Add everything to your slow cooker and add some pepper and salt.
2. Cook on low for eight hours.
3. Add more salt and pepper if needed before serving.

Nutrition Facts Per Serving

- Calories: 244 kcal
- Carbohydrates: 46.8 g
- Dietary Fiber: 13.4 g
- Protein: 13.77 g
- Fat: 13.8 g
- Saturated Fat: 0.26 g

43

CREOLE OKRA CORN SOUP

Serves: 6

Prep Time: 15 minutes

Cook Time: 7 hours

Ingredients

- ½ white onion, minced
- 3 garlic cloves, minced
- 6 oz sliced okra
- 28 oz crushed tomatoes
- 1 cup corn
- 3 cups vegetable broth
- ½ green pepper, minced
- 1 tsp oregano
- 1 tsp marjoram
- ½ tsp cayenne pepper
- Salt and pepper to taste

Directions

1. Place all of the ingredients in your slow cooker and mix them together.
2. Cook on low for seven hours.
3. Once done, add pepper and salt to taste.

Nutrition Facts Per Serving

- Calories: 154 kcal
- Carbohydrates: 32.27 g
- Dietary Fiber: 4.7 g
- Protein: 5.27 g
- Fat: 1.7 g
- Saturated Fat: 0.24 g

44

MORROCAN CHICKPEA SOUP
WITH KALE

This is literally a set-it-and-forget-it recipe. All you have to do is chop the veggies and then add everything to the slow cooker. Your slow cooker will handle the rest! What can be easier than that?

Serves: 6

Prep Time: 15 minutes

Cook Time: 6 hours

Ingredients

- 2 (15 oz) cans chickpeas, drained
- 1 (15 oz) can diced tomatoes
- 1 small yellow onion, chopped
- 2 cloves garlic, minced
- 2 medium carrots, chopped

- 2 cups kale leaves, chopped
- 4 cups vegetable broth
- ½ tsp ground cumin
- ½ tsp ground ginger
- ½ tsp ground cinnamon

Directions

1. Add everything to your slow cooker and stir well.
2. Cover and cook on low for six hours.
3. Once done, taste and season with some pepper and salt if needed.
4. Serve with cooked quinoa.

Nutrition Facts Per Serving

- Calories: 250 kcal
- Carbohydrates: 40.6 g
- Dietary Fiber: 11.6 g
- Protein: 11.2 g
- Fat: 5.8 g
- Saturated Fat: 0.56 g

45

LENTIL SOUP

Lentils, potatoes, and carrots make this recipe healthy, warming and filling. It's easy to prepare, making it perfect for busy weeknights.

Serves: 4

Prep Time: 5 minutes

Cook Time: 7 hours

Ingredients

- 1 cup green lentils
- ½ onion, fincly chopped
- 2 cloves garlic, minced
- 1 medium carrot, chopped
- 1 cup potatoes, chopped
- 1 cup vegetable broth

- 5 cups water
- 1 tsp thyme
- Salt and pepper to taste

Directions

1. Add everything to your cooker and set to cook for seven hours on low.
2. When done, add pepper and salt to taste.

Nutrition Facts Per Serving

- Calories: 90 kcal
- Carbohydrates: 18.8 g
- Dietary Fiber: 2.7 g
- Protein: 4.2 g
- Fat: 0.7 g
- Saturated Fat: 0.13 g

46

SPLIT PEA SOUP

Serves: 3

Prep Time: 5 minutes

Cook Time: 7 hours

Ingredients

- 1 cup split peas
- 2 small carrots, peeled and diced
- 1 medium potato, peeled and diced
- 3 cups vegetable broth
- 1 tsp turmeric
- 1 tsp thyme
- ¼ tsp roscmary

Directions

1. Place everything in your cooker and mix together.
2. Cook on low for seven hours.
3. Add pepper and salt to taste.

Nutrition Facts Per Serving

- Calories: 370 kcal
- Carbohydrates: 67.7 g
- Dietary Fiber: 21.4 g
- Protein: 21.9 g
- Fat: 2.9 g
- Saturated Fat: 0.5 g

BUTTERNUT SQUASH SOUP

Serves: 4

Prep Time: 15 minutes

Cook Time: 6 hours

Ingredients

- 1 butternut squash, diced
- 3 medium carrots, peeled and chopped
- 1 medium onion, chopped
- 2 (14 oz) cans vegetable broth
- 2 cups water
- ¼ tsp ground nutmeg
- ¼ tsp cinnamon
- Salt and pepper to taste

Directions

1. Add butternut squash, carrots, and onion to your slow cooker and add in the broth and water.
2. Cover and cook on low for six hours.
3. When done, use an immersion blender to puree everything until smooth. Add nutmeg and cinnamon. Stir.
4. Taste and add pepper and salt if needed.
5. Enjoy.

Nutrition Facts Per Serving

- Calories: 158 kcal
- Carbohydrates: 40g
- Dietary Fiber: 7g
- Protein: 3.47g
- Fat: 0.47g
- Saturated Fat: 0.12g

48

ITALIAN BEAN SOUP

This is another soup that is full of healthy whole food. A quick and truly satisfying Italian bean soup, a perfect comfort food.

Serves: 6

Prep Time: 10 minutes

Cook Time: 5 hours

Ingredients

- 1 onion, chopped
- 2 ribs celery, chopped
- 3 carrots, peeled and chopped
- 1 lb dry Great Northern beans
- 1 tbsp fennel seeds
- 2 (14 oz) cans vegetable broth

119

- 1 (14 oz) can crushed tomatoes
- 1 cup water
- 2 tsp Italian seasoning
- 2 tsp garlic powder
- Salt and pepper to taste

Directions

1. Add onion, carrots, celery, beans to your slow cooker.
2. Add the garlic powder, Italian seasonings, and fennel seeds.
3. Add broth and water. Cover and cook on five hours on high.
4. If needed, add more water to get the thickness you like. Taste and add pepper and salt.

Nutrition Facts Per Serving

- Calories: 292 kcal
- Carbohydrates: 55g
- Dietary Fiber: 17.7g
- Protein: 17.75g
- Fat: 1.19g
- Saturated Fat: 0.3g

49

LENTIL SOUP WITH POTATOES AND CHARD

Serves: 6

Prep Time: 10 minutes

Cook Time: 8 hours

Ingredients

- 2 cloves garlic, minced
- 1 yellow onion, chopped
- 1 cup dried brown lentils, rinsed
- 2 carrots, sliced
- 3 potatoes, chunked
- 1 bunch Swiss chard, stems and leaves sliced
- 6 cups vegetable broth
- 1 tbsp soy sauce

Directions

1. Place all ingredients in the slow cooker. Stir.
2. Cover and cook on low for eight hours.
3. When done, stir well to make sure everything is well incorporated.
4. Taste and add pepper and salt if needed.

Nutrition Facts Per Serving

- Calories: 211 kcal
- Carbohydrates: 43.3g
- Dietary Fiber: 5.9g
- Protein: 6.72g
- Fat: 2.45g
- Saturated Fat: 0.3g

50

VEGAN GUMBO

This recipe will bring a bit of southern flavor to your vegan kitchen. Feel free to substitute any vegetables you have on hand.

Serves: 6

Prep Time: 20 minutes

Cook Time: 8 hours

Ingredients

- 2 tbsp all-purpose flour
- 1 ycllow onion, chopped
- 2 cloves garlic, minced
- 1 green bell pepper, chopped
- 2 carrots, diced

- 1 (14.5 oz) can diced tomatoes
- 1 (15 oz) can kidney beans, rinsed
- 1 cup frozen sliced okra
- 3 cups vegetable broth
- 1 tbsp Cajun seasoning
- 1 tbsp thyme

Directions

1. Add everything except flour to the slow cooker. Stir.
2. Cover and cook on low for eight hours.
3. When done, take two tablespoons liquid out of the slow cooker and mix well with the flour. Then, pour it back into the slow cooker.
4. Remove the lid and allow it to thicken for about 30 minutes. If the gumbo is too thick, add more water or broth.
5. Taste. Add pepper and salt if needed.
6. Serve over brown rice.

Nutrition Facts Per Serving

- Calories: 107 kcal
- Carbohydrates: 26.31g

- Dietary Fiber: 2.6g
- Protein: 3.47g
- Fat: 4.14g
- Saturated Fat: 1.1g

51

GREAT NORTHERN BEAN AND KALE STEW

Serves: 8

Prep Time: 10 minutes

Cook Time: 8 hours

Ingredients

- 1 lb dried Great Northern Beans, rinsed
- 1 yellow onion, finely chopped
- 2 cloves garlic, minced
- 1 large carrot, peeled and diced
- 1 cup baby kale, finely chopped
- 1 (14 oz) can diced tomatoes
- 5 cups water or vegetable broth
- 1/2 tsp oregano
- 1/2 tsp thyme
- 1/2 tsp rosemary
- 1 tbsp salt

- Black pepper to taste

Directions

1. Add all ingredients except tomatoes and kale to the slow cooker.
2. Cover and cook on low for seven hours.
3. When beans are soft, add tomatoes, kale, salt, and pepper and let cook for another one hour.
4. Serve.

Nutrition Facts Per Serving

- Calories: 273 kcal
- Carbohydrates: 47g
- Dietary Fiber: 13.6g
- Protein: 15.24g
- Fat: 3.15g
- Saturated Fat: 0.65g

52

FIRE ROASTED CHILI

Serves: 8

Prep Time: 15 minutes

Cook Time: 8 hours

Ingredients

- 28 oz fire roasted tomatoes
- 3 tbsp tomato paste
- 2 cloves garlic, minced
- 1 yellow onion, diced
- ½ red bell pepper, seeded and chopped
- ½ poblano pepper, seeded and chopped
- 1 (15 oz) can pinto beans, rinsed and drained
- 1 (15 oz) can kidney beans, rinsed and drained
- 1 ½ cups vegetable broth

- ½ tbsp chili powder
- Salt and pepper to taste
- 1 avocado, chopped (for topping)

Directions

1. Add all ingredients except avocados to the slow cooker. Stir.
2. Cover and cook on low for eight hours.
3. When done, stir well to make sure everything is well incorporated.
4. Taste. Add pepper and salt if needed.
5. Top with chopped avocado and enjoy!

Nutrition Facts Per Serving

- Calories: 188 kcal
- Carbohydrates: 28g
- Dietary Fiber: 8.6g
- Protein: 8.8g
- Fat: 5.8g
- Saturated Fat: 0.9g

VI

BEANS & GRAINS

53

SPANISH RICE

Also known as Mexican rice, this is one of the most simple recipes to prepare and has a great flavor.

Serves: 8

Prep Time: 5 minutes

Cook Time: 3 hours

Ingredients

- 2 cups long grain rice
- ½ cup chopped onion
- 2 garlic cloves, minced
- ½ cup yellow bell pepper, chopped
- ½ cup red bell pepper, chopped
- 1 (14.5 oz) can diced tomatoes, drained
- 2 cups water

- 1 tsp chili powder
- ½ tsp cumin
- ½ tsp salt

Directions

1. Lightly coat the slow cooker with olive oil.
2. Add everything to your cooker and stir well. Cover and cook on high for three hours.
3. When done, check the rice. It should be tender and the liquid should be absorbed.
4. Fluff the rice with a fork.

Nutrition Facts Per Serving

- Calories: 81 kcal
- Carbohydrates: 16.7 g
- Dietary Fiber: 1.3 g
- Protein: 2.17 g
- Fat: 0.7 g
- Saturated Fat: 0.1 g

VEGAN JAMBALAYA

This vegan jambalaya recipe is full of fresh produce. It's super easy to make with basic pantry staples, making it a hearty and warming recipe for busy weeknights.

Serves: 6

Prep Time: 10 minutes

Cook Time: 6 hours

Ingredients

- 2 cups long grain rice
- 3 garlic cloves, minced
- 1 onion, diced
- 2 celery stalks, diced

- 1 bell pepper, diced
- 1 cup tomatoes, diced
- 1 (14 oz) can red kidney beans, drained
- 4 cups vegetable broth
- 1 cup water
- 1 tsp thyme
- 1 tsp oregano
- 1 tsp paprika

Directions

1. Add four cups of broth and all the ingredients, except for the rice and kidney beans, to your cooker. Set on low for four hours.
2. Next, mix in the rice and one cup water. Switch to high and cook for 2 hours. Rice should be tender and the liquid absorbed when done.
3. Mix in the beans and enjoy!

Nutrition Facts Per Serving

- Calories: 314 kcal
- Carbohydrates: 64.8 g
- Dietary Fiber: 7.1 g

- Protein: 9.47 g
- Fat: 2.22 g
- Saturated Fat: 0.4 g

55

MAPLE BAKED BEANS

Serves: 6

Prep Time: 10 minutes

Cook Time: 5 hours

Ingredients

- 1 (15 oz) can navy beans, drained
- 1 (15 oz) can kidney beans, drained
- 3 garlic cloves, crushed
- ½ tsp grated ginger
- 1 onion, finely diced
- 1 tbsp apple cider vinegar
- ¼ cup tomato paste
- 1 tbsp mustard
- ½ cup maple syrup
- ½ tsp salt

Directions

1. Rinse the beans and place them in your cooker.
2. Mix all the other ingredients and stir well.
3. Cook for five hours on high. Make sure you stir often, so it does not burn. Enjoy.

Nutrition Facts Per Serving

- Calories: 229 kcal
- Carbohydrates: 47 g
- Dietary Fiber: 7.6 g
- Protein: 9.92 g
- Fat: 0.91 g
- Saturated Fat: 0.2 g

56

SPICY BLACK-EYED PEAS

Serves: 6

Prep Time: 20 minutes

Cook Time: 4.5 hours

Ingredients

- 1 ½ cups dried black-eyed peas
- 2 garlic cloves, minced
- 1 small onion, chopped
- 1 bell pepper, diced
- 5 cups vegetable broth
- 1 tsp mustard
- 2 tsp Tabasco
- 1 tsp salt

Directions

1. Rinse and sort the peas and get rid of stones and dirt. Combine everything in your cooker. Set to 4 ½ hours on high. Stir a few times to make sure everything gets distributed.
2. This can be served immediately or frozen.

Nutrition Facts Per Serving

- Calories: 185 kcal
- Carbohydrates: 34.9 g
- Dietary Fiber: 7.9 g
- Protein: 10.87 g
- Fat: 0.76 g
- Saturated Fat: 0.18 g

57

RED BEANS AND RICE

Serves: 4

Prep Time: 10 minutes

Cook Time: 6 hours

Ingredients

- 2 (15 oz) cans red beans, rinsed and drained
- 3 garlic cloves, minced
- 1 small yellow onion, chopped
- 1 cup celery, chopped
- 1 cup brown rice, rinsed
- 3 cup vegetable broth
- 2 tsp thyme
- ¼ tsp cayenne pepper
- 1 tsp paprika

Directions

1. Combine everything, except for the rice, in the cooker. Cook for four hours on low.
2. Mix in the rice and some pepper and salt. Switch to high for another two hours. Enjoy.

Nutrition Facts Per Serving

- Calories: 320 kcal
- Carbohydrates: 58 g
- Dietary Fiber: 9.6 g
- Protein: 14.2 g
- Fat: 4.06 g
- Saturated Fat: 0.6 g

MUSHROOM RISOTTO

Risotto is one of those dishes that we love to eat, but seldom have the patience to make. However, with a slow cooker, you can just prepare the ingredients and let it do its magic.

Serves: 6

Prep Time: 15 minutes

Cook Time: 1.5 hours

Ingredients

- 4 tbsp olive oil
- 1 clove garlic, minced
- ¼ onion, diced
- 8 oz portabella mushrooms, sliced
- 1 ¾ cup Arborio rice

- 1 (15 oz) can sweet peas, drained
- 4 cups vegetable broth
- Pepper and salt

Directions

1. Add olive oil to a pot and sauté the garlic, mushrooms, and onions. Stir in the rice, cooking for two minutes.
2. Coat your cooker with nonstick spray and pour in the rice.
3. Add the broth, pepper, and salt. Set to high for 1 ½ hours. Mix in the peas when done. Enjoy!

Nutrition Facts Per Serving

- Calories: 358 kcal
- Carbohydrates: 59 g
- Dietary Fiber: 5.8 g
- Protein: 7.95 g
- Fat: 10.03 g
- Saturated Fat: 1.4 g

HERBED BROWN RICE

Serves: 4

Prep Time: 10 minutes

Cook Time: 3 hours

Ingredients

- 2 tbsp vegan butter
- 2 cup long grain brown rice
- 1 (8 oz) can sliced mushrooms, drained
- 3 cups vegetable broth
- ½ tsp oregano
- ½ tsp thyme
- Pepper and salt to taste

Directions

1. In a skillet, melt the vegan butter and add in the rice. Cook for four minutes.
2. Add the rice to the cooker with the oregano, thyme, broth, and mushrooms. Mix everything together.
3. Cover and cook on high for three hours.
4. Add pepper and salt to taste.

Nutrition Facts Per Serving

- Calories: 418 kcal
- Carbohydrates: 76.4 g
- Dietary Fiber: 3.9 g
- Protein: 9.17 g
- Fat: 8.66 g
- Saturated Fat: 4.2 g

60

BLACK BEANS

Serves: 8

Prep Time: 10 minutes

Cook Time: 3.5 hours

Ingredients

- 1 lb black beans, rinsed
- 1 onion, chopped
- 3 garlic cloves, crushed
- 6 cups water
- 1 tsp cumin
- 1 bay leaf
- Pepper and salt to taste

Directions

1. Place black beans, onion, garlic, cumin, and bay leaf in a slow cooker.
2. Add water.
3. Cook on high for 3.5 hours, and then test doneness.
4. Remove the bay leaf and garlic cloves.
5. Add salt and pepper to taste.

Nutrition Facts Per Serving

- Calories: 208 kcal
- Carbohydrates: 37.6 g
- Dietary Fiber: 9.2 g
- Protein: 12.6 g
- Fat: 0.9 g
- Saturated Fat: 0.2 g

61

VEGAN GRITS

This is a wonderful vegan grits recipe that is great for a creamy tasty breakfast or side dish.

Serves: 6

Prep Time: 5 minutes

Cook Time: 7 hours

Ingredients

- 4 cups water
- 1 cup stone-ground grits
- 1 tbsp olive oil
- 1 tbsp coconut oil
- Salt to taste

Directions

1. Spray inside your slow cooker with cooking spray.
2. Mix all of the ingredients together in your cooker.
3. Cook on low for seven hours. The grits are ready once thickened and creamy.
4. Add more salt if needed.
5. Enjoy!

Nutrition Facts Per Serving

- Calories: 116 kcal
- Carbohydrates: 16.6 g
- Dietary Fiber: 1 g
- Protein: 1.6 g
- Fat: 4.8 g
- Saturated Fat: 2.3 g

62

BBQ BAKED BEANS

Serves: 8

Prep Time: 10 minutes

Cook Time: 7 hours

Ingredients

- 1 white onion, diced
- 3 garlic cloves, minced
- 4 cups vegetable broth
- 3 cups dried great northern beans
- 1 cup favorite BBQ sauce
- Sea salt to taste

Directions

1. Soak the beans overnight in water.
2. Add all of the ingredients to your cooker.

3. Cook on low for seven hours.
4. Taste and add any extra seasonings if needed.

Nutrition Facts Per Serving

- Calories: 255 kcal
- Carbohydrates: 48.15 g
- Dietary Fiber: 14 g
- Protein: 15.7 g
- Fat: .86 g
- Saturated Fat: 0.26 g

63

CUBAN BLACK BEANS

Serves: 8

Prep Time: 5 minutes

Cook Time: 8 hours

Ingredients

- 1 lb black beans, rinsed and soaked overnight
- 3 garlic cloves, minced
- 1 white onion, diced
- 1 jalapeno pepper, diced
- 1 green bell pepper, diced
- 6 cups water
- 2 tbsp olive oil
- Juice of 1 lime
- ½ tsp cumin
- 2 tsp salt

Directions

1. Add all ingredients except for the lime juice to the slow cooker.
2. Cover and cook on low for eight hours.
3. Once done, add the lime juice and enjoy.

Nutrition Facts Per Serving

- Calories: 235 kcal
- Carbohydrates: 38.2 g
- Dietary Fiber: 9.2 g
- Protein: 12.65 g
- Fat: 4.25 g
- Saturated Fat: 0.7 g

VEGAN CHARRO BEANS

The word "charro" actually means Mexican horseman or cowboy, and this why you might see this recipe titled "Cowboy Beans." With a slow cooker, you can enjoy this hearty taste of the South even more easily!

Serves: 8

Prep Time: 10 minutes

Cook Time: 7 hours

Ingredients

- 1 lb dried Pinto beans, rinsed
- 4 garlic cloves, minced
- ½ yellow onion, diced
- 1 (15 oz) can diced tomatoes

- 4 cups water
- 2 cups vegetable broth
- 1 cup cilantro, chopped
- ½ tsp cumin
- 1 tsp chili powder
- Salt and black pepper to taste

Directions

1. Add everything except the tomatoes and cilantro to your slow cooker and stir well. Cook for seven hours on low.
2. Mix in the tomatoes and cover, cooking for another hour.
3. Top with chopped cilantro and season with some pepper and salt to taste before serving.

Nutrition Facts Per Serving

- Calories: 222 kcal
- Carbohydrates: 39.8 g
- Dietary Fiber: 10.2 g
- Protein: 12.9 g
- Fat: 1.53 g
- Saturated Fat: 0.2 g

SWEET BOURBON BAKED BEANS

Serves: 8

Prep Time: 10 minutes

Cook Time: 10 hours

Ingredients

- 1 lb. dried pinto beans
- ½ onion, finely chopped
- 1 cup bourbon
- ½ cup brown sugar
- ½ cup maple syrup
- 1 tbsp olive oil
- 1 tbsp vegan Worcestershire sauce
- 1 tbsp mustard
- 4 tbsp ketchup
- Salt and pepper to taste

Directions

1. Mix all of the ingredients together in your slow cooker.
2. Cover and set the slow cooker to cook for ten hours on low. Once done, add pepper and salt to taste.

Nutrition Facts Per Serving

- Calories: 332 kcal
- Carbohydrates: 66.2 g
- Dietary Fiber: 9.1 g
- Protein: 12.5 g
- Fat: 2.4 g
- Saturated Fat: 0.4 g

VII

CURRY

66

BUTTERNUT SQUASH LENTIL CURRY

Serves: 8

Prep Time: 15 minutes

Cook Time: 8 hours

Ingredients

- 1 medium butternut squash, peeled and cubed
- 2 cups red lentils
- 2 cloves garlic, minced
- 2 tbsp ginger, grated
- 1 (13.5 oz) can coconut milk
- 3 cups vegetable stock
- 1 tsp curry powder
- ½ tsp cumin
- ½ tsp coriander
- ½ tsp turmeric

Directions

1. Place all of the ingredients in your cooker and mix together.
2. Cover and cook for eight hours on low.
3. Enjoy.

Nutrition Facts Per Serving

- Calories: 351 kcal
- Carbohydrates: 47.4g
- Dietary Fiber: 8.9 g
- Protein: 15.02 g
- Fat: 13.4 g
- Saturated Fat: 10.4 g

67

CHANA MASALA

As one of the most well-known dishes in the world, both in and out of India and Pakistan, channa masala is chickpeas cooked with a spicy tomato-based sauce. Serve it with your favorite rice for a heart-warming lunch or dinner!

Serves: 4

Prep Time: 20 minutes

Cook Time: 5 hours

Ingredients

- 1 (29 oz) can chickpeas, drained
- 1 medium yellow onion, chopped
- 4 cloves garlic, minced
- 1 tbsp ginger, grated

- 1 tbsp olive oil
- 2 cups vegetable broth
- 2 tbsp tomato paste
- 2 tbsp chana masala powder (or garam masala)
- 1 tsp cayenne
- ½ tsp turmeric
- ½ tsp cumin
- ½ tsp salt

Directions

1. Sauté the onion and ginger with olive oil in a pot over medium heat until onion is browned, about 5-7 minutes. Mix in the garlic, chana masala, cayenne, turmeric, cumin, and salt. Cook until fragrant.
2. Place in the slow cooker along with the rest of the ingredients.
3. Cover and cook for five hours on high. Check occasionally and add water if needed.
4. Serve with rice.

Nutrition Facts Per Serving

- Calories: 168 kcal

- Carbohydrates: 20.9 g
- Dietary Fiber: 5.1 g
- Protein: 5.4 g
- Fat: 7.7 g
- Saturated Fat: 0.9 g

68

COCONUT QUINOA CURRY

Serves: 6

Prep Time: 20 minutes

Cook Time: 4 hours

Ingredients

- ½ medium onion, diced
- 2 cloves garlic, minced
- 1 tbsp ginger, grated
- 2 small sweet potato, chopped
- 1 broccoli crown, cut into florets
- ¼ cup quinoa
- 1 (15 oz) can chickpeas, rinsed and drained
- 1 (14.5 oz) cans coconut milk
- 2 cups water
- 3 tsp tamari
- 1 tsp turmeric

- 1 tsp curry powder

Directions

1. Place everything in your cooker with 2 cups of water. Stir well.
2. Cover and set for four hours on high. Check occasionally and add water if needed.
3. The sweet potato should be soft when done.

Nutrition Facts Per Serving

- Calories: 300 kcal
- Carbohydrates: 30.6 g
- Dietary Fiber: 8.5 g
- Protein: 9.3 g
- Fat: 17.86 g
- Saturated Fat: 14 g

69

ALOO GOBI

Aloo gobi is a delicious Indian dish in which cauliflower and potatoes are cooked with onions, tomatoes, and spices. It is a side dish that is so simple yet surprisingly good.

Serves: 4

Prep Time: 10 minutes

Cook Time: 4 hours

Ingredients

- 3 tbsp olive oil
- 1 tbsp ginger, grated
- 1 clove garlic, minced
- 1 head cauliflower, diced
- 2 medium potatoes, peeled and cubed

- 2 tomatoes, diced
- ¼ cup low sodium vegetable stock
- 1 tsp turmeric
- 1 tsp cumin
- 1 tbsp garam masala
- ½ tsp cayenne

Directions

1. Place the oil, ginger, garlic, all the spices and salt at the base of the slow cooker.
2. Add the rest of the ingredient to the slow cooker.
3. Cover and cook for four hours on high.
4. Serve with some cilantro and rice.

Nutrition Facts Per Serving

•Calories: 270 kcal

•Carbohydrates: 39.9 g

•Dietary Fiber: 6.5 g

•Protein: 5.95 g

•Fat: 10.85 g

•Saturated Fat: 1.6 g

70

CREAMY CHICKPEAS TOFU CURRY

Serves: 4

Prep Time: 20 minutes

Cook Time: 4 hours

Ingredients

- 1 (15 oz) can chickpeas, rinsed and drained
- 12 oz firm tofu, drained and cubed
- 1 small yellow onion, diced
- 4 cloves garlic, minced
- ½ tsp ginger
- 2 tbsp olive oil
- 1 cup tomato purcc
- 1 cup coconut milk
- 1 tbsp curry powder
- 1 tbsp garam masala
- 1 tsp chili powder

Directions

1. Heat oil in a pot over medium-high heat. Add the onion and cook for 3-4 minutes. Add garlic, ginger, chili powder, curry powder, garam masala and sauté for another 2 minutes.
2. Add tomato puree and coconut milk, and let cook for about five minutes over low heat. Add salt and pepper to taste.
3. Add the cubed tofu and chickpeas in the slow cooker. Pour in the sauce. Cook for 5 hours on low.
4. Serve with rice.

Nutrition Facts Per Serving

- Calories: 367 kcal
- Carbohydrates: 28.8 g
- Dietary Fiber: 8.4 g
- Protein: 16 g
- Fat: 23.8 g
- Saturated Fat: 13 g

71

CAULIFLOWER LENTIL THAI CURRY

These curry lentils are really easy to make. You basically just throw all the ingredients into the pot and let it simmer until the lentils and veggies are cooked. This is a dish that is satisfying, filling, comforting and delicious, and it is high in plant-based protein and fiber.

Serves: 5

Prep Time: 15 minutes

Cook Time: 6 hours

Ingredients

- 1 head cauliflower, diced
- ½ yellow onion, chopped
- 3 cloves garlic, minced

- 1 cup red lentils
- 2 tbsp Thai curry paste
- 3 cups vegetable broth
- ⅔ cup coconut milk
- 1 tsp ginger powder
- 1 tsp turmeric

Directions

1. Coat the slow cooker with cooking spray.
2. Add all the ingredients, except the coconut milk in the cooker. Stir.
3. Cook for six hours on low.
4. Once done, mix in the coconut milk and let it cook for another 15 minutes.
5. Serve with rice and enjoy!

Nutrition Facts Per Serving

- Calories: 268 kcal
- Carbohydrates: 36.8 g
- Dietary Fiber: 7.9 g
- Protein: 11.6 g
- Fat: 10 g
- Saturated Fat: 7.2 g

72

GREEN LENTIL CURRY

Serves: 4

Prep Time: 10 minutes

Cook Time: 8 hours

Ingredients

- 1 small yellow onion, diced
- 1 ½ cup green lentils, rinsed
- 3 tbsp tomato paste
- 2 ½ cup water
- 1 (13.5 oz) can coconut milk
- 2 tsp garam masala
- 2 tsp brown sugar
- 3 tsp curry powder
- ½ tsp ginger powder
- 1 tsp garlic powder

Directions

1. Add all the ingredients to the slow cooker. Stir well.
2. Cover and set for eight hours on low.
3. Serve over rice.

Nutrition Facts Per Serving

- Calories: 276 kcal
- Carbohydrates: 19.1 g
- Dietary Fiber: 4.1 g
- Protein: 5.7 g
- Fat: 22.4 g
- Saturated Fat: 19 g

VEGETABLE CURRY

Serves: 4

Prep Time: 10 minutes

Cook Time: 6 hours

Ingredients

- 1 small yellow onion, diced
- 2 sweet potatoes, peeled and diced
- 1 cup water
- 1 (8.5 oz) can mixed vegetables (carrots, corn, green beans, and peas), drained
- 1 (13.5 oz) can coconut milk
- 1 tsp garam masala
- 1 tsp turmeric
- 1 tsp garlic powder
- 1 tsp ginger powder

Directions

1. Mix all of the spices together in a bowl. Add the coconut milk and stir.
2. Add the onion, sweet potatoes, veggies to the slow cooker and pour in the coconut milk of the previous step.
3. Set for five hours on low. Serve with rice.

Nutrition Facts Per Serving

- Calories: 302 kcal
- Carbohydrates: 25.4 g
- Dietary Fiber: 6.4 g
- Protein: 4.4 g
- Fat: 22.2 g
- Saturated Fat: 19 g

74

TROPICAL PINEAPPLE AND MANGO CURRY

Pineapple, mango, and coconut all in one dish? Yes, sign me up! This is a recipe that can't go wrong and will win everyone's heart.

Serves: 6

Prep Time: 15 minutes

Cook Time: 4 hours

Ingredients

- 1 cup fresh mango, diced
- 1 cup fresh pineapple, diced
- ½ white onion, diced
- 2 cloves garlic, minced
- 1 cup water
- 2 (13.5 oz) cans coconut milk

- 2 tsp curry powder
- 2 tsp cumin
- 2 tsp brown sugar
- 1 tsp ginger powder
- ½ tsp cinnamon

Directions

1. Combine everything in your cooker.
2. Cook for four hours on high. Check occasionally and add water if needed.
3. Serve with rice.

Nutrition Facts Per Serving

- Calories: 366 kcal
- Carbohydrates: 23.3 g
- Dietary Fiber: 4.4 g
- Protein: 3.9 g
- Fat: 31.5 g
- Saturated Fat: 27 g

VIII

STAND-ALONE SUPPERS

75

MEXICAN QUINOA TACOS

Serves: 6

Prep Time: 5 minutes

Cook Time: 3 hours

Ingredients

- 1 cup quinoa
- 1 (15 oz) can corn
- 1 (14.5 oz) can diced tomatoes
- 1 (30 oz) can black beans
- 10 oz enchilada sauce
- 3 tbsp taco seasoning
- 1 cup vegetable broth

Directions

1. Rinse the quinoa before placing it in the

slow cooker. Add everything else to the slow cooker and stir well.

2. Cover and set for three hours on high. Once the quinoa is cooked, serve the mixture on tortillas and top with your favorite toppings.

Nutrition Facts Per Serving

- Calories: 378 kcal
- Carbohydrates: 67 g
- Dietary Fiber: 15.2 g
- Protein: 17.6 g
- Fat: 5.5 g
- Saturated Fat: 1.4 g

VEGAN LENTIL BOLOGNESE

Serves: 5

Prep Time: 15 minutes

Cook Time: 9 hours

Ingredients

- 4 cloves garlic, minced
- ¼ yellow onion, chopped
- 3 tomatoes, sliced
- 1 eggplant, chopped
- 1 head cauliflower, chopped
- 1 cup lentils
- 1 ½ cup vegan pasta
- 3 cups water
- ¼ cup olive oil
- 3 cups tomato sauce
- 3 tbsp Italian seasoning

- Salt to taste

Directions

1. Add the lentils to your cooker and add the oil.
2. Place the eggplant in the cooker, along with the tomato sauce.
3. Add the cauliflower, garlic, onion, Italian seasoning, and some salt to the cooker.
4. Pour in 3 cups of water.
5. Lay the tomatoes over the top and place on the lid. Cook for nine hours on low. You can stir the mixture occasionally.
6. Cook the pasta according to package directions. Add to the slow cooker and give everything a good stir. Enjoy!

Nutrition Facts Per Serving

- Calories: 268 kcal
- Carbohydrates: 36.5 g
- Dietary Fiber: 9.7 g
- Protein: 6.84 g
- Fat: 12.5 g
- Saturated Fat: 1.7 g

TEMPEH BRAISED WITH FIGS

This recipe combines the flavor of port wine with fresh figs and nutty tempeh. Serve it with healthy vegan mashed potatoes and sea-salted asparagus for a sophisticated vegan dish!

Serves: 4

Prep Time: 15 minutes

Cook Time: 7 hours

Ingredients

- 8 figs, cut into wedges
- 8 oz tempeh, cubed
- 1 small onion, minced
- 1 clove garlic, minced
- 1 tbsp vegan bouillon

- 1 tbsp balsamic vinegar
- 1 cup port wine
- ½ cup water
- 1 sprig thyme

Directions

1. Cook the onions and garlic in a skillet until fragrant.
2. Next, place the cooked onions, garlic, the figs, and tempeh in a container.
3. Store in the refrigerator overnight.
4. The following day, mix everything together in your cooker. Place on the lid and set for seven hours on low.

Nutrition Facts Per Serving

- Calories: 168 kcal
- Carbohydrates: 19.5 g
- Dietary Fiber: 2 g
- Protein: 11.6 g
- Fat: 6.3 g
- Saturated Fat: 1.2 g

RATATOUILLE

Enjoy this classic Provençal stew of tomatoes, zucchini, eggplant, and peppers with this easy slow cooker recipe without being tied to the kitchen!

Serves: 6

Prep Time: 20 minutes

Cook Time: 7 hours

Ingredients

- 3 cloves garlic, smashed
- 2 onions, cut in half and sliced
- 3 tomatoes, chunked
- 3 zucchini, chunked
- 2 eggplant, chunked
- 4 bell peppers, chunked

- 4 tbsp olive oil
- 2 tbsp tomato paste
- 3 tbsp balsamic vinegar
- 1 tsp dried basil
- 1 tsp oregano
- Salt and pepper to taste

Directions

1. Place everything in your slow cooker. Stir well.
2. Cover and cook for 7 hours on low. Make sure to stir at least once. The vegetables should be extremely tender.
3. Drizzle with more olive oil before serving if desired.

Nutrition Facts Per Serving

- Calories: 168 kcal
- Carbohydrates: 20.2 g
- Dietary Fiber: 7.3 g
- Protein: 3.67 g
- Fat: 9.6 g
- Saturated Fat: 1.3 g

BELL PEPPER MUSHROOM PASTA

This bell pepper mushroom pasta recipe is so easy to make and tastes delicious that it will soon become your go-to meal on a budget!

Serves: 4

Prep Time: 15 minutes

Cook Time: 2 hours

Ingredients

- ½ medium yellow onion, diced
- 2 cloves garlic, minced
- 3 cups diced tomatoes
- 1 green pepper, chopped
- 1 red pepper, chopped
- 5 sliced mushrooms

- 2 cups water
- 2 tbsp Italian seasoning
- 2 cups vegan pasta
- 1 tbsp olive oil
- Salt to taste

Directions

1. Add everything except for the pasta to your cooker and mix together.
2. Cover and cook on high for 2 hours. The vegetables should be tender.
3. Mix in the pasta during the last 25 minutes. Add some water if needed to cover the pasta. Make sure to stir well.
4. Add salt to taste. Drizzle with 1 tbsp olive oil before serving if desired.
5. Enjoy.

Nutrition Facts Per Serving

- Calories: 170 kcal
- Carbohydrates: 30.4 g
- Dietary Fiber: 5.9 g
- Protein: 3.9 g
- Fat: 4.2 g
- Saturated Fat: 0.58 g

CORN CHOWDER

Serves: 6

Prep Time: 10 minutes

Cook Time: 3.5 hours

Ingredients

- ½ medium yellow onion, finely chopped
- 1 clove garlic, minced
- 2 medium potatoes, peeled and chopped into 1-inch pieces
- 1 medium sweet potato, peeled and chopped into 1-inch pieces
- 2 cups frozen corn
- 3 cups vegan stock
- 1 (14 oz) can coconut milk
- 1 tsp salt
- ½ tsp pepper

- Chopped green onions or chives

Directions

1. Combine the potatoes, onion, garlic, salt and vegan stock in your slow cooker. Cover and cook on high for 3 hours, or until the potatoes are very tender.
2. Using an immersion blender, blend until creamy.
3. Add corn and the coconut milk and cook for another 20 minutes.
4. Add salt and pepper to taste.
5. Serve with chopped green onions or chives.

Nutrition Facts Per Serving

- Calories: 352 kcal
- Carbohydrates: 43 g
- Dietary Fiber: 6.2 g
- Protein: 8.9 g
- Fat: 17.5 g
- Saturated Fat: 14.3 g

81

VEGGIE FAJITAS

Fajitas are pretty easy to make. When you make them with a slow cooker, it is even easier! Try this recipe, you won't be disappointed!

Serves: 2

Prep Time: 10 minutes

Cook Time: 3 hours

Ingredients

- 1 tbsp olive oil
- 1 medium yellow onion, sliced
- 3 bell peppers, sliced
- 1 cup cherry tomatoes, halved
- 1 tsp paprika
- 1 tsp hot chili powder

- 1 tsp cumin
- ½ tsp coriander
- ½ pepper
- 1 avocado, sliced (for topping)
- Chopped cilantro (for topping)

Directions

1. Add everything except for the tomatoes to your cooker. Cover and cook for 2 hours on high.
2. Next, mix in the tomatoes and cook for another one hour.
3. Serve the veggies on a tortilla with your favorite toppings.

Nutrition Facts Per Serving

- Calories: 216 kcal
- Carbohydrates: 36.6 g
- Dietary Fiber: 6 g
- Protein: 4.8 g
- Fat: 8.13 g
- Saturated Fat: 1.14 g

82

QUINOA AND VEGGIES

There are so many benefits of quinoa. It is one of the most protein-rich foods we can eat. Also, it contains almost twice as much fiber as most other grains. I started to replace the rice with quinoa and I find that it is really a perfect substitute that is yummy and more nutritious.

Serves: 4

Prep Time: 10 minutes

Cook Time: 7 hours

Ingredients

- 1 medium yellow onion, chopped
- 2 cloves garlic, minced
- 1 red pepper, chopped

- 1 carrot, peeled and chopped
- 1 ½ cups quinoa
- 2 tbsp olive oil
- 3 cup vegetable broth
- ¼ tsp pepper
- Chopped cilantro

Directions

1. Rinse your quinoa and then place it in the cooker. Add some olive oil to coat the quinoa.
2. Add the garlic, onion, pepper, carrot, and the broth.
3. Place on the lid and cook for 7 hours on low.
4. Fluff the quinoa and stir in the cilantro before serving.

Nutrition Facts Per Serving

- Calories: 346 kcal
- Carbohydrates: 48.1 g
- Dietary Fiber: 5.5 g
- Protein: 9.7 g
- Fat: 13.07 g
- Saturated Fat: 1.7 g

BLACK BEAN STUFFED PEPPERS

These black bean stuffed peppers may look difficult to prepare, but as you make them, you will find them extremely easy to make. It is definitely a quick, easy and satisfying meal!

Serves: 6

Prep Time: 15 minutes

Cook Time: 6 hours

Ingredients

- 1 (14 oz) can refried beans
- 1 (14 oz) can black beans, rinsed
- 6 bell peppers
- ½ cup quinoa, rinsed
- ½ cup red enchilada sauce

- ½ tsp cumin
- 1 tsp garlic salt
- 1 tsp onion powder
- 1 tsp chili powder
- 1 tsp paprika

Directions

1. Cut the tops off the peppers, and remove the seeds and ribs.
2. Mix all the other ingredients together in a large bowl and fill the peppers with the mixture.
3. Add ½ cup of water to your cooker and place the peppers in the cooker.
4. Cover and cook for six hours on low.
5. Enjoy!

Nutrition Facts Per Serving

- Calories: 213 kcal
- Carbohydrates: 37.2 g
- Dietary Fiber: 9.6 g
- Protein: 11.5 g
- Fat: 2.8 g
- Saturated Fat: 0.6 g

ENCHILADA QUINOA

Serves: 6

Prep Time: 10 minutes

Cook Time: 4 hours

Ingredients

- 1 (15 oz) can black beans, rinsed
- 1 (15 oz) can fire-roasted tomatoes
- 1 (15 oz) can yellow corn, rinsed
- 2 (15 oz) cans red enchilada sauce, divided
- 1 cup quinoa
- ½ cup water
- ¼ tsp pepper
- 4 oz vegan shredded cheese
- 1 tsp salt
- Optional toppings: Sliced green onions,

avocado, diced tomatoes, chopped cilantro, and lime wedges

Directions

1. Add quinoa, tomatoes, 1 can enchilada sauce, corn, and beans to your slow cooker and stir.
2. Pour the other can of enchilada sauce on top and then sprinkle the vegan cheese.
3. Cover and cook for four hours on high.
4. Serve with your favorite toppings.

Nutrition Facts Per Serving

- Calories: 365 kcal
- Carbohydrates: 53.2 g
- Dietary Fiber: 9.7 g
- Protein: 18.6 g
- Fat: 10.4 g
- Saturated Fat: 4.6 g

85

VEGAN BBQ JACKFRUIT

With its "meaty" texture and taste, this tasty BBQ jackfruit recipe will quickly become your favorite sandwich filling!

Serves: 6

Prep Time: 10 minutes

Cook Time: 3 hours

Ingredients

- 1 clove garlic, minced
- 1 white onion, diccd
- 3 (14 oz) cans jackfruit, drain and rinsed
- ½ cup vegan BBQ sauce
- ½ cup vegetable broth

Directions

1. Add the jackfruit, garlic, and onion to the slow cooker.
2. Pour the BBQ sauce and vegetable broth over the top and stir to distribute evenly.
3. Cover and cook for three hours on high.
4. Once done, shred the jackfruit with two forks.
5. Serve with burger buns and enjoy.

Nutrition Facts Per Serving

- Calories: 205 kcal
- Carbohydrates: 49.8 g
- Dietary Fiber: 3.7 g
- Protein: 4.01 g
- Fat: 1.37 g
- Saturated Fat: 0.4 g

86

ASIAN GARLIC TOFU

Tofu is a very important source of protein for many vegan people. It goes very well with an Asian flavor. This flavorful garlic tofu will change the impression you have of tofu! (If you didn't like it before.)

Serves: 2

Prep Time: 10 minutes

Cook Time: 8 hours

Ingredients

- 2 (14 oz) packages extra firm tofu, drained and diced
- 2 cloves garlic, minced
- 1 carrot, chopped
- 1 tbsp freshly grated ginger

- 4 tbsp soy sauce
- 1 tsp sesame oil
- 1 tbsp agave
- ½ cup water
- green onions for garnish

Directions

1. Combine the following ingredients in a small bowl: garlic, ginger, water, soy sauce, sesame oil, and agave.
2. Add the tofu and the carrot to the slow cooker.
3. Pour the sauce on top of everything.
4. Cover and cook for eight hours on low.
5. Top with chopped green onions and serve.

Nutrition Facts Per Serving

- Calories: 237 kcal
- Carbohydrates: 9.7 g
- Dietary Fiber: 1.8 g
- Protein: 20.82 g
- Fat: 14.9 g
- Saturated Fat: 1.6 g

IX

DESSERTS

HOT FUDGE CHOCOLATE CAKE

Serves: 6

Prep Time: 15 minutes

Cook Time: 2 hours

Ingredients

- 1 cup AP flour
- ¼ cup cocoa powder
- 1 tsp baking powder
- ½ cup brown sugar
- ½ tsp salt
- 1 tsp vanilla extract
- ¾ cup almond milk
- ⅓ cup olive oil
- 2 cups hot fudge
- 1 cup vegan chocolate chips

Directions

1. Place a liner into your cooker for easy cleanup.
2. Mix the flour, cocoa powder, baking powder, sugar, and salt together.
3. Stir in the vanilla, olive oil, and almond milk. Once well combined, pour the batter into your cooker.
4. Sprinkle the top with chocolate chips.
5. Heat the chocolate fudge in the microwave until pourable. Pour the cake batter in, and make sure you do not stir.
6. Place the lid on and cook on high for an hour. Check the cake to see if it is done. If a toothpick does not come out clean, set it for another 30 minutes.
7. Let cool for ten minutes.
8. Serve the cake with some vegan ice cream.

Nutrition Facts Per Serving

- Calories: 552 kcal
- Carbohydrates: 94 g
- Dietary Fiber: 3.1 g
- Protein: 6.7 g

- Fat: 17.6 g
- Saturated Fat: 4.6 g

APPLE QUINOA CRISP

This apple quinoa crisp has healthy ingredients such as apple, coconut oil, quinoa, oats, and cinnamon. On top of that, it tastes delicious and your kids will love it!

Serves: 4

Prep Time: 10 minutes

Cook Time: 2.5 hours

Ingredients

- 6 apples, cored and sliced
- 5 tbsp coconut oil
- 1 cup oats
- 1 cup quinoa

- 2 tbsp coconut flour
- 2 tsp cinnamon, divided
- ¾ cup coconut sugar, divided
- Pinch salt

Directions

1. In a large bowl, add ½ cup of sugar and a teaspoon of cinnamon. Add the apple slices to the bowl and toss to combine.
2. Move the apples to the bottom of your cooker.
3. In the same bowl, stir together the remaining cinnamon and sugar, coconut flour, quinoa, oats, and salt.
4. Add the coconut oil, and stir well. Sprinkle this over the top of the apples.
5. Cover and set for two hours on high. Once the time is up, take the lid off and let it cook for another 30 minutes.
6. Serve with some vegan ice cream.

Nutrition Facts Per Serving

- Calories: 580 kcal
- Carbohydrates: 100 g

- Dietary Fiber: 13.9 g
- Protein: 10.8 g
- Fat: 21.7 g
- Saturated Fat: 15.4 g

89

PEACH COBBLER

Serves: 8

Prep Time: 15 minutes

Cook Time: 5 hours

Ingredients

Filling:

- 6 cups sliced peaches
- 2 tbsp maple syrup
- ¼ tsp nutmeg
- 2 tsp cinnamon
- Pinch salt

Topping:

- 2 cups AP flour

- 3 tsp baking powder
- 1 tbsp brown sugar
- 1 tsp salt
- ¾ cup almond milk
- ¼ cup vegan butter

Directions

1. Add all of the filling ingredients to your slow cooker.
2. Mix the baking powder, flour, sugar, and salt together in a large bowl. Once mixed, add in the vegan butter and almond milk. Mix well.
3. Spoon the topping over the peaches.
4. Cover and cook for 5 hours on low. The topping should be firm when done.
5. Serve with vegan ice cream. Enjoy!

Nutrition Facts Per Serving

- Calories: 349 kcal
- Carbohydrates: 72.8 g
- Dietary Fiber: 3.8 g
- Protein: 4.34 g
- Fat: 6.59 g
- Saturated Fat: 3.7 g

90

SLOW COOKER BAKED APPLE

Serves: 8

Prep Time: 15 minutes

Cook Time: 2 hours

Ingredients

- 8 apples, cored and sliced into rings
- 1 tbsp vegan butter
- 1 cup apple juice
- ¼ tsp vanilla extract
- 1 tsp ginger powder
- 1 tsp cinnamon
- ½ tsp nutmcg
- 2 tbsp brown sugar

Directions

1. Lay sliced apple in the bottom of the slow cooker. Add brown sugar and cinnamon and stir until apple are coated evenly.
2. Add the vegan butter, vanilla, and apple juice. Stir well.
3. Mix the spices and sugar in a small bowl and then sprinkle the mixture over the apple slices.
4. Place on the lid and cook for two hours on high.
5. Serve with your favorite vegan ice cream.

Nutrition Facts Per Serving

- Calories: 140 kcal
- Carbohydrates: 32.9 g
- Dietary Fiber: 4.6 g
- Protein: .54 g
- Fat: 1.85 g
- Saturated Fat: 0.9 g

91

CINNAMON PECANS

These sweet, delicious and healthy slow cooker cinnamon pecans make great holiday gifts. It's a treat enjoyed by people of all ages and it's super easy to make.

Serves: 8

Prep Time: 10 minutes

Cook Time: 3.5 hours

Ingredients

- ¼ cup almond milk
- 3 tsp vanilla
- 4 cups pecan halves
- 3 tbsp cinnamon
- 1 cup brown sugar

- ¼ tsp salt

Directions

1. Whisk together the vanilla and almond milk in a medium bowl.
2. Mix the cinnamon, salt, and sugar in another bowl.
3. Place the pecans into the vanilla mixture and then roll them in the cinnamon mixture. Place the pecans into your cooker.
4. Cover and cook on low for 3.5 hours. Make sure you stir every 30 minutes. Once the time is up, allow them to cool before serving.
5. Serve or keep in a container.

Nutrition Facts Per Serving

- Calories: 462 kcal
- Carbohydrates: 37.1 g
- Dietary Fiber: 4.74 g
- Protein: 7.58 g
- Fat: 35.7 g
- Saturated Fat: 3.06 g

92

PINEAPPLE UPSIDE DOWN CAKE

Serves: 10

Prep Time: 15 minutes

Cook Time: 3 hours

Ingredients

- 10 maraschino cherries, stems removed
- 1 (20 oz) can pineapple slices in juice, drained, juice reserved
- 1 cup all-purpose flour
- ¼ cup vegan butter, melted
- ¼ cup vegetable oil
- ½ cup applesauce
- ¾ tsp baking powder
- 1 cup brown sugar
- 1 tsp cinnamon
- ½ teaspoon salt

Directions

1. Coat the slow cooker with some non-stick spray.
2. Combine the brown sugar and vegan butter and pour in the slow cooker.
3. Lay the pineapple slices into the cooker. Do not overlap.
4. Set a cherry into the center of each pineapple slice.
5. Combine the flour, baking powder, cinnamon, and ½ teaspoon salt in a medium bowl.
6. Add oil, pineapple juice, and applesauce to the bowl and mix well. Pour this over your pineapple.
7. Place on the lid and set for three hours on high. Let the cake cool a bit before serving.

Nutrition Facts Per Serving

- Calories: 234 kcal
- Carbohydrates: 35.72 g
- Dietary Fiber: 0.8 g
- Protein: 1.4 g
- Fat: 10.2 g
- Saturated Fat: 7.4 g

93

MAPLE SYRUP BROWN RICE PUDDING

This recipe uses resistant starch-rich brown rice instead of white rice. All you need is five ingredients and 3 hours to make this creamy, tasty and healthy dessert!

Serves: 4

Prep Time: 5 minutes

Cook Time: 3 hours

Ingredients

- 1 stick cinnamon
- ⅔ cup brown rice, rinsed
- ¼ cup maple syrup
- 1 tsp vanilla
- 32 oz almond milk

Directions

1. Place everything in your cooker and stir well.
2. Cover and set for three hours on high.
3. At this point, it should be a thick pudding. If not, cook a bit longer.
4. Remove the cinnamon stick before serving.

Nutrition Facts Per Serving

- Calories: 307 kcal
- Carbohydrates: 48.2 g
- Dietary Fiber: 1.1 g
- Protein: 9.6 g
- Fat: 8.2 g
- Saturated Fat: 2.4 g

94

SEA SALT CHOCOLATE ALMOND CLUSTERS

Serves: 12

Prep Time: 5 minutes

Cook Time: 30 minutes

Ingredients

- 1 tsp sea salt
- 2 ½ cups almonds
- 12 oz dark vegan chocolate chips
- 1 tsp vanilla

Directions

1. Place all of the ingredients in your cooker and mix them together.
2. Cover and cook on low for 30 minutes.
3. Make sure you stir the mixture every 10

minutes so the chocolate won't burn and become stiff.

4. Use an ice cream scoop to place dollops of the mixture on wax paper. Sprinkle the top with some sea salt. Place them in the fridge until firm. Enjoy!

Nutrition Facts Per Serving

- Calories: 320 kcal
- Carbohydrates: 12.51 g
- Dietary Fiber: 4.5 g
- Protein: 7.5 g
- Fat: 22.7 g
- Saturated Fat: 4.2 g

95

RICE PUDDING

Serves: 4

Prep Time: 10 minutes

Cook Time: 2.5 hours

Ingredients

- ¾ cup long-grain white rice, rinsed
- 1 tsp vanilla
- 2 tbsp coconut oil
- 4 cups almond milk
- 1 tsp cinnamon
- ½ cup brown sugar

Directions

1. Mix all of the ingredients into your cooker, stirring until the sugar melts.

2. Place the lid on and cook on high for two and a half hours.
3. Stir again when done, and enjoy.

Nutrition Facts Per Serving

- Calories: 414 kcal
- Carbohydrates: 77.9 g
- Dietary Fiber: 1.8 g
- Protein: 4.1 g
- Fat: 10.04 g
- Saturated Fat: 5.9 g

X

HOT DRINKS

96

MULLED CRANBERRY CIDER

This mulled cranberry hot cider is warming and delicious. It's not too sweet, which makes it a perfect holiday cocktail.

Serves: 8

Prep Time: 10 minutes

Cook Time: 4 hours

Ingredients

- 3 (5-inch) rosemary sprigs
- 3 cinnamon sticks
- 2 tbsp whole cloves
- 1 orange
- 1 cup cranberries
- ¼ cup agave nectar

- 8 cups apple cider

Directions

1. Pour the apple cider into your slow cooker. Stir the agave nectar into the cider.
2. Stud the orange with the cloves. Set the orange into the cider, and add the rosemary, cinnamon sticks, and cranberries.
3. Cover and cook for low for 3-4 hours.
4. Strain the cider through a mesh sieve. Pour the liquid back into the slow cooker to keep warm. Garnish with fresh cranberries and rosemary sprigs.

Nutrition Facts Per Serving

- Calories: 161 kcal
- Carbohydrates: 39.5 g
- Dietary Fiber: 3.3g
- Protein: 0.74g
- Fat: 0.63g
- Saturated Fat: 0.17 g

97

ORANGE-CRANBERRY MULLED WINE

Serves: 6

Prep Time: 15 minutes

Cook Time: 3 hours

Ingredients

- 1 orange
- 2 cups orange juice
- ⅓ cup brown sugar
- ⅓ cup brandy
- 2 cinnamon sticks
- 2 tbsp whole cloves
- 1 cup fresh cranberries
- 1 bottle Merlot

Directions

1. Place the sugar, cranberries, orange juice, and wine into your slow cooker. Stir until the sugar dissolves.
2. Clean the orange well and then stud it with the whole cloves. Place the orange into the wine along with the cinnamon sticks.
3. Cover and cook for low to 3 hours.
4. Once done, take the cinnamon sticks and orange out carefully, and then strain the wine through a sieve.
5. Add the wine back into the cooker and mix in the brandy. Add extra sugar if you need to.
6. Serve in a glass with an orange slice and cinnamon stick. Enjoy!

Nutrition Facts Per Serving

- Calories: 257 kcal
- Carbohydrates: 34.53 g
- Dietary Fiber: 0.9g
- Protein: 1.03g
- Fat: 0.39 g
- Saturated Fat: 0.12 g

PUMPKIN GINGERBREAD LATTE WITH ALMOND MILK

Serves: 6

Prep Time: 10 minutes

Cook Time: 2 hours

Ingredients

- ⅓ cup pumpkin puree
- ¼ cup maple syrup
- 1 tsp vanilla extract
- 3 tbsp instant espresso
- 6 cups almond milk
- 1 cinnamon stick
- 2 tsp ground ginger
- ¾ tsp ground nutmeg

Directions

1. Add everything to the cooker and mix them together.
2. Place on the lid and set for 2 hours on low. It shouldn't boil, but it should get hot.
3. Once done, switch the cooker to warm. Make sure you stir so that it does not scald.
4. Serve with some cinnamon or nutmeg.

Nutrition Facts Per Serving

- Calories: 198 kcal
- Carbohydrates: 33.05 g
- Dietary Fiber: 1.5 g
- Protein: 3.53 g
- Fat: 6.33 g
- Saturated Fat: 0.65 g

99

PEPPERMINT MOCHA

This recipe is great for a December morning beverage. Make this peppermint mocha, grab a blanket and a book and enjoy!

Serves: 4

Prep Time: 5 minutes

Cook Time: 2 hours

Ingredients

- 4 tsp instant espresso powder
- ¾ cup vegan chocolate chips
- ¼ cup peppermint syrup
- 4 cups almond milk

Directions

1. Add everything to the slow cooker and stir well.
2. Place on the lid and cook for 2 hours on low. Stir the mixture so that the chocolate is distributed evenly.
3. Serve with some vegan chocolate shavings.

Nutrition Facts Per Serving

- Calories: 280 kcal
- Carbohydrates: 29.8 g
- Dietary Fiber: 5.2 g
- Protein: 5.12 g
- Fat: 15.96 g
- Saturated Fat: 8 g

100

SPICED APPLE CIDER

Serves: 8

Prep Time: 10 minutes

Cook Time: 4 hours

Ingredients

- 8 cups apple cider
- 1 medium orange
- 2 tbsp cloves
- 3 cinnamon sticks

Directions

1. Add the cider and the cinnamon sticks to your cooker.
2. Poke the cloves into the skin of the orange and place the orange into the cider.

3. Place on the lid and cook for four hours on low. Serve with a splash of rum.

Nutrition Facts Per Serving

- Calories: 123 kcal
- Carbohydrates: 30.2 g
- Dietary Fiber: 0.9 g
- Protein: 0.41 g
- Fat: 0.35 g
- Saturated Fat: 0.06 g

AFTERWORD

I sincerely hope that you have enjoyed the recipes and the information found in this book.

A plant-based diet full of seeds, nuts, legumes, beans, whole grains, vegetables, and fruits is beneficial for your health as well as the environment. While making the transition may seem difficult, just remember everything you will be reaping when you make the change. I know you'll love the benefits.

Because your diet will be full of these healthy foods, you will be consuming a higher amount of fiber, phytochemicals, minerals, and vitamins. You will be consuming an abundant amount of iron, magnesium, folic acid, and vitamins E, C, and B1, while not eating as much cholesterol.

As a vegan, you will be reducing your risk of obesity, stroke, hypertension, ischemic heart disease, cardiovascular disease, type-2 diabetes, and cancer. These are just the beginning of the benefits you will get from a plant-based diet as you learned in the first chapter.

I hope you the most in your new healthy lifestyle. You will not ever regret making this healthy switch to a vegan diet, and you will be amazed at how amazing you feel afterward.

Finally, if you found this book useful in any way, a review on Amazon is always appreciated!

AUTHOR'S NOTE

Thank you so much for taking the time to read my book. I hope you have enjoyed reading this book as much as I've enjoyed writing it. If you enjoyed this book, please consider leaving a review on Amazon. Your support really means a lot and keeps me going.

If you have any questions, please don't hesitate to contact me at ask@cleaneatingspirit.com

Don't forget to follow me on Facebook for more information related to health and wellness.

cleaneatingspirit.com/

Printed in Great Britain
by Amazon

53973743R00166